PRAISE FOR *FAIRNESS IS OVERRATED*

Whether you are a business leader trying to integrate your faith into your work or a pastor who wants to step up to another level of leadership, *Fairness Is Overrated* will give you the handles you need.

—PERRY NOBLE, FOUNDING AND SENIOR PASTOR OF
NEWSPRING CHURCH, SOUTH CAROLINA

Tim Stevens has written a guide to leadership and life that comes in bite-size portions but offers deep and hard-fought wisdom. You'll feel like you're having a conversation with a leader worth following. Because you will be.

—JOHN ORTBERG, BEST-SELLING AUTHOR, SPEAKER, AND SENIOR
PASTOR OF MENLO PARK PRESBYTERIAN CHURCH, CALIFORNIA

Fairness Is Overrated gets past the surface, all the way down to the core of what matters in the heart of a leader. The principles Tim writes about won't produce a here-today-gone-tomorrow leader, but one who can confidently lead with integrity for the long haul. Get this book into the hands of every business leader in your church.

—MARK BATTERSON, *New York Times* BEST-SELLING
AUTHOR OF *The Circle Maker* AND LEAD PASTOR OF
NATIONAL COMMUNITY CHURCH, WASHINGTON, DC

Fairness Is Overrated is an incredible leadership book for those in the workplace. Tim Steven's principles are timeless; their application is life-changing. Business leaders, church leaders, all leaders: get this book and devour it immediately!

—THOM S. RAINER, AUTHOR OF *I Am a Church
Member* AND *Autopsy of a Deceased Church*

If you need to find the right team, build a healthy staff culture, or lead through challenging times, then pick up this book.

—PETE WILSON, AUTHOR OF *Plan B* AND FOUNDING AND SENIOR
PASTOR OF CROSS POINT CHURCH, NASHVILLE, TENNESSEE

Fairness Is Overrated is packed with powerful wisdom that will equip business and ministry leaders with the tools to successfully lead their organizations.

—CRAIG GROESCHEL, FOUNDER AND
SENIOR PASTOR OF LIFECHURCH.TV

Tim Stevens is a leader's leader and leader of leaders. He not only talks about it, but actually does it. Smart leadership is both theory and practice, and *Fairness Is Overrated* provides both. This book is practical, helpful, applicable, and time-tested. Whether a pastor or CEO, this book will help you be a better leader. I highly recommend it.

—BRAD LOMENICK, AUTHOR OF
The Catalyst Leader AND *H3 Leadership*

Tim Stevens is a voice of wisdom to which every church leader should be listening. His writing has been invaluable to my leadership development. *Fairness Is Overrated* is another collection of practical, direct, concise, and essential leadership lessons that you'll want to share with your team and revisit often.

—JENNI CATRON, CHURCH LEADER AND AUTHOR OF
Clout: Discover and Unleash Your God-Given Influence

I'm not objective. I'm a big enough fan of Tim Stevens that I hired him to run a key division in our company. Having said that, it's the wisdom in this book that caused me to hire him. It's not fair for me to recommend Tim's work, but fairness is overrated. Buy the book. You won't be sorry.

—WILLIAM VANDERBLOEMEN, PRESIDENT OF
VANDERBLOEMEN SEARCH GROUP

I had the privilege of working with Tim for more than eight years. He was my boss and remains a great friend. In other words, I'm guessing I know Tim better than you know Tim. The leadership principles he writes about in *Fairness Is Overrated* really work. I know, because I experienced them firsthand.

—TONY MORGAN, FOUNDER AND CHIEF STRATEGIC
OFFICER OF THE UNSTUCK GROUP

Every page and every chapter of this book is grounded in the heart of a man who leads well every day. Read this and become a better leader.

—Dr. John Jackson, president of William Jessup University, speaker, and author

Fairness Is Overrated is a fantastic read that quickly gets to the point of the qualities of an effective leader. Tim's book is an essential read for any leader at any level, whether you are leading a few or a few thousand.

—Joel Gates, president of Gates Automotive Group

Tim Stevens nails the essence of how to create and maintain a business culture that will sustain over the long term. *Fairness Is Overrated* does an unbelievable job of mapping out all the essentials in developing a successful business culture where leaders can thrive which ultimately helps everything else that makes a business successful fall right into place.

—Jason D. Lippert, chairman and CEO of Lippert Components, Inc

There is no one I know more qualified to write about or speak on the topic of leadership than Tim Stevens. He is not only a gifted leader of people but also a proven leader of leaders. If you are just entering the arena of leadership or if you are a seasoned leader with a desire to take your skills to the next level, this book is absolutely a must read.

—Joel A. Mikell, president of RSI Stewardship

Tim is as efficient and to the point in business matters as he is in his writings. His quick wit and sense of humor makes him a delight to work with as well as read. This book should be used as a handbook that is never more than arm's length away from ministers regardless of the size of their church.

—W. Dennis Moses, vice president and national business manager of Bank of the West, Religious Institutional Banking

I have read lots of books on leadership over the years but I cannot remember one that is as practical day-to-day as *Fairness Is Overrated*. These are timeless principles written in an easy to understand way. Get your marker and pen out before you read this book—you are going to make notes all over the place! And you will be a far better leader for having done so.

—Jim Sheppard, CEO and principal of GENERIS
and coauthor of *Contagious Generosity*

Tim Stevens could have written either a survival guide for people in ministry or a success guide. This book is both! I found it very useful, as well as winsome and inspirational.

—Dr. Joel C. Hunter, senior pastor of
Northland—A Church Distributed

FAIRNESS IS OVERRATED

AND 51 OTHER LEADERSHIP PRINCIPLES TO REVOLUTIONIZE YOUR WORKPLACE

TIM STEVENS

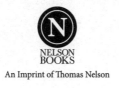

NELSON BOOKS

An Imprint of Thomas Nelson

Published in Nashville, Tennessee, by Nelson Books, an imprint of Thomas Nelson. Nelson Books and Thomas Nelson are registered trademarks of HarperCollins Christian Publishing, Inc.

Author is represented by the Blythe Daniel Agency, P.O. Box 64197, Colorado Springs, CO 80920.

Interior designed by James A. Phinney.

Thomas Nelson, Inc., titles may be purchased in bulk for educational, business, fund-raising, or sales promotional use. For information, please e-mail SpecialMarkets@ThomasNelson.com.

Unless otherwise noted, Scripture quotations are taken from the Holy Bible, New International Version®, NIV®. Copyright © 1973, 1978, 1984, 2011 by Biblica, Inc.™ Used by permission of Zondervan. All rights reserved worldwide. www.zondervan.com

Scripture quotations marked ESV are from THE ENGLISH STANDARD VERSION. © 2001 by Crossway Bibles, a division of Good News Publishers.

Scripture quotations marked MSG are from *The Message* by Eugene H. Peterson. © 1993, 1994, 1995, 1996, 2000. Used by permission of NavPress Publishing Group. All rights reserved.

Scripture quotations marked NLT are from *Holy Bible*, New Living Translation. © 1996, 2004. Used by permission of Tyndale House Publishers, Inc., Wheaton, Illinois 60189. All rights reserved.

978-0-7180-2192-4 (IE)

Library of Congress Cataloging-in-Publication Data

Stevens, Tim, 1967-
 Fairness is overrated : and 51 other leadership principles to revolutionize your workplace / Tim Stevens.
  pages cm
 Includes bibliographical references and index.
 ISBN 978-1-4002-0654-4 (alk. paper)
 1. Leadership--Religious aspects--Christianity. I. Title.
 BV4597.53.L43S746 2014
 158'.4--dc23
                              2013050890

Printed in the United States of America
15 16 17 18 19 RRD 6 5 4 3 2 1

CONTENTS

CONTENTS

INTRODUCTION

I DIDN'T LIKE MIDDLE SCHOOL. IN FACT, I CAN'T THINK OF anything good that happened during those three years. I'm sure I learned, passed tests, played in band concerts, and such, but it was an awkward time. I was changing from a boy to a man; from being a class clown to wanting to be more; from the kid the teachers begged the principal *not* to put in their classes (yes, literally) to someone who was going to make a difference with his life. And the transition was difficult and ugly.

I hadn't been in high school long when I walked into Miss Wessel's class. She had always been a bit intimidating to me. Maybe it's because she typically wore a gray polyester skirt and a blue blazer; maybe it's because she was so intense; or maybe it's because she had no time for kids who weren't serious, and I was still figuring out how to be serious.

I was a sophomore in high school when Miss Wessel began to teach me about leadership. Little did I know, she had her eyes on me for several years and saw potential in me, and as soon as I was in her class, she began to teach me how to be a leader.

Some of what she taught me was related to systems, structures, and strategies. And that turned out to be helpful. I became the class president a year later and then the school president my senior year. But the stuff that really marked me was what she taught me about leadership from the life of Nehemiah.[1] I remember going through her classes with my heart beating fast—I was discovering how God had wired me. As Rick Warren explained it, I was finding my purpose—the reason I was put on this earth.[2]

I learned how this guy, Nehemiah, was able to make an impact on a country and bring hope and change—all by leveraging his influence. Nehemiah got a vision from God, delegated, loved people, showed compassion, conducted research, developed strategy, motivated, persevered through hard times, dealt with critics, and resolved conflict.

But what I most identify with about Nehemiah is that he wasn't the king. He wasn't the president or captain. In fact, when he started, he wasn't in charge of anything. He was just the guy who would sip the king's wine to see if it was poisonous. He had the king's trust, but in some ways, he was the most expendable guy in the kingdom. Yet he didn't let his lowly position stop him from leading.

We've all met people who use their supposed lack of position as an excuse not to lead. I have listened to people complain about "the management" while not lifting a finger to help. I have watched associates gossip and gripe rather than propose a solution. It's always easy to sit around and do nothing while pointing a finger at someone else.

I could easily have become just another complaining, finger-pointing employee, but Miss Wessel ignited within me an unquenchable desire to learn, a vision that I could make a difference, and the tools to get started on my leadership journey.

That was thirty years ago, and I'm still on the journey. Every day I sharpen my skills or learn new ways to be an effective leader. The journey, which began with Miss Wessel, continued when I was asked, as an eighteen-year-old, to manage a production team as it traveled across the country performing in school auditoriums, churches, and civic centers. I learned about systems, communication, and leading people who were older and more experienced than I was. It expanded when, as a twenty-three-year-old, I became part of the leadership team for that national nonprofit group and began to learn about leveraging my influence on an entire organization.

Some people thought I had taken a few steps backward when, at twenty-seven, I left the stability of a great job and tremendous responsibility to join the team of a start-up church that had no building and only a few hundred people. But over the next fifteen years, we saw that little church grow to become a ministry reaching thousands, and it was even voted in a national poll as the second most innovative church in America.[3] My leadership had to bend and morph as the organization grew more complex. When I left in 2014, it had more than one hundred employees, multiple campuses, spin-off organizations, church-planting initiatives, a restaurant, and a preschool.

I've learned that leading smart doesn't just happen. It requires tenacity, a learner's heart, some mentors, a boatload of experience, and humility to get back up when you fail. I don't claim to be an expert leader, but I've always been committed to passing along whatever I learn. This book is my effort to pour what I have learned about leadership into one place. My goal is for this to be a manual you will reach for again and again as you face new challenges.

Two Groups of Leaders

There are some specific leaders who have been on my mind and in my prayers as I have been writing. If you find yourself in one of these two groups (or if you hope to be in one of them), then you will find much of the information in this book relevant to your specific situations:

CHURCH LEADERS

Because I spent the last twenty years as a church leader, my heart beats with and for you. I think leadership in a church is as complex as it gets. Leading people is difficult for any executive, but when you sprinkle a bit of discipleship and theology in the mix, it pegs the difficulty meter into the red zone. I've written six books, including the one you are now reading, and taught more than twenty-five thousand church leaders because of my passion to help pastors get this right. This book is for you, not because I am the expert, but because I am learning along with you.

BUSINESS LEADERS

Because my feet have remained squarely planted in a local church, business leaders surround me. I have wonderful opportunities to mentor business leaders and help them work through leadership issues. Every week I have engaging conversations with friends who are on their own leadership journeys in the marketplace. From business owners to entrepreneurs to managers to punch-the-clock, hourly workers, I love coming alongside business leaders to help them think through conflict resolutions and strategies or refine their visions.

Four Leadership Skills

As I worked on this project, certain skills began to emerge that are crucial for any leader to learn at any level of the organization. You will find the pages that follow organized around these four categories of leadership thought:

PART ONE: BE A LEADER WORTH FOLLOWING

It all starts right here. Nothing more can be said or should be said about leadership until we deal with the person in the mirror.

Because leaders are sometimes isolated, they convince themselves they won't be seen. Since they have paid their dues working up to their positions, they can fall into "exceptional" thinking—believing they are the exception, and the normal rules don't apply to them.

This is a section about having the right guardrails in your life—not so you will look more spiritual, but so you can lead with strength in a way that is right and honorable. The right leaders with appropriate boundaries will elevate the shape of the organization and keep the culture from being dragged down by needless accusations or scandals.

PART TWO: FIND THE RIGHT PEOPLE

The success of a leader will rise or fall on the decisions he or she makes about the people around him or her. A culture will not and cannot be positive without solid hiring decisions. It is true for every leader at any level. Whether you are a chief executive, the senior pastor, or the person in charge of a department, your greatest leadership challenge is surrounding yourself with the right people (this includes volunteers). It doesn't matter how gifted a leader is; if he doesn't have the right people around him, representing him and pulling with him, his leadership potential will eventually be capped.

Just as important as picking the right people is making the tough decision to release a person when a bad choice has been made. Christians struggle with this. Bill Hybels said Christian leaders have a case of "terminal niceness."[4] We want to be full of grace, and so sometimes our organizations limp along because we won't make the right staffing decisions. And delaying these decisions sinks a culture faster than just about anything else.

PART THREE: BUILD A HEALTHY CULTURE

Every leader is developing a culture through everyday decisions, whether intentionally or not. Culture happens. With focus and skill, any organization can have a great culture where people are standing in line to join the team, where team members are energized by the mission, and where it's not just a job—people actually *do life* together.

On the other hand, a culture that is ignored will begin to turn into a cesspool of gossip, fear, turnover, and unhealthy competition. This is the natural way of any organization with more than a few human beings working in it. Healthy leaders are intent on employing simple strategies to nurture a great culture. And this happens through intentional daily decisions, learned skills, and practiced principles.

PART FOUR: LEAD CONFIDENTLY THROUGH A CRISIS

Most of the time you will be leading day to day in normal conditions. It won't be unusually hard or unusually easy. It will be just another day. And there will be thousands of days like this. (I was a leader at Granger Community Church for more than seven thousand days, and probably six thousand of them were fairly normal.)

But every leader who stays with an organization for very long will eventually face a crisis. It might be one that impacts a small department, or it might be big enough that it has the potential to take down the entire organization. Many leaders buckle under such pressure.

It doesn't matter so much how great you are at leading your department or ministry when the sun is shining and everything is working. That's pretty simple. The question is how well you will do when the opposite is true. It's leading through a crisis that separates great leaders from mediocre leaders. You can't wait until the crisis comes to think about the essential skills you'll need to get you to the other side.

Every leader, director, or manager in any church, business, or organization has the potential to shape the culture and influence the heart and soul of the organization. My passion is to help you develop the skills and discover the tools of leadership to revolutionize your workplace, starting from your circle of influence out to the entire organization. *Fairness Is Overrated* challenges the leader first to look in the mirror, then to consider how to build an effective team, and finally to develop critical skills and behaviors that are required for a winning culture.

How to Use This Book

I'm big on questions: What kind of leader are you? Do you talk more than you listen? Do you have a hard time leading people who are not like you? Do you delay while you strive for fairness when you really should make a decision and move on? Do you allow meetings to get out of control, which in turn makes no one want to attend your meetings? Do you chew people out when they make mistakes? Are you a secure leader or an insecure leader? Are you okay when the people below you know more than you do?

Because questions are so important, I've included a couple at the end of every chapter. I encourage you to go through the book with a discussion group, a leadership team, or a gathering of businesspeople. Take time to talk through the questions I've provided or make up your own. The greatest leadership lessons come when you have to wrestle an idea to the ground. Whether or not you agree with me, it's a win if something I say creates room for your team to have a productive discussion.

As I mentioned before, this book is categorized into the four main parts of leadership tools described earlier. You may want to go through the book sequentially. You may wish to jump around based on your current challenges. If you are working through this as a team, perhaps you'll pick a chapter to go through at the beginning of every meeting over the next year.

However you decide to tackle this book, this is my prayer:

Father, there are leaders who have this book in their hands right now, and each one is coming from a different place. Perhaps she is discouraged and ready to quit. Perhaps he is young and has no idea how to get started. Perhaps she has succumbed to temptation and is trying to find her way back. I ask you to use these words, along with the guidance of your Holy Spirit, and revive the hearts of your people. Give them a new vision for their leadership and influence. Call them to a life of character and integrity. Give them the endurance to withstand the stresses and trials they face, and let them see a glimpse of what can happen when they commit their leadership and direction to you. Amen.

PART ONE

BE A LEADER WORTH FOLLOWING

MY EARLIEST MEMORY OF A LEADER FALLING WAS WHEN I was in seventh grade. I remember looking out my bedroom window to see two of the pastors from our church walking up to our house. They didn't look happy. I found out later they were visiting all the families who had students in Mr. Jackson's sixth-grade class. He had molested some of my friends, and my favorite teacher was suddenly gone.

A few years later another teacher at my school was found to be in an inappropriate relationship with a high school student. During that same year, there were two national Christian leaders who fell quite publicly. I don't know whether it started becoming an epidemic in the mideighties or if I was just coming of age and aware of it for the first time. But it seems as if it has snowballed since then.

In recent years, several of my good friends have been taken out of the game because of personal choices. Each time it breaks my heart. I hate losing friends. I hate having to be involved in a decision to end their employment because they didn't live up to the standard of a leader. I hate having to console others through their pain while dealing with my own. I hate thinking back over my time with one of those friends and realizing some of it was built on deception. The pain of betrayal is real, and it happens way too often.

In my world, everyone enjoys a good talk about leadership. We love to go to conferences to hear about a church that is being innovative or listen to a leader who has built an organization from nothing, seemingly overnight. We pay money to learn how to grow our youth ministries, put on more effective services, or get more people in small groups. We eat up the stories of church leaders who think outside the lines to draw crowds. And we lean in when someone says, "Forget the crowds. There is a better way to make disciples."

In your world, it might be workshops on improving sales, increasing profits, or doing a better job with guest relations. The bottom line is often the driving concern.

And yet just about every week we hear of another leader who has fallen. It might be having an affair, stealing money, lying to a client, participating in sexual deviance, or something else that takes him or her out of the game. But the person is sidelined, even if for a season, because of personal choices.

When witnessing the falls of some of these leaders, people around me sometimes have responded with haughty shock or judgmental anger. I typically become quiet because I realize I am not immune. I am just a few bad choices away from being in the same boat.

It's exactly for that reason I write this section. Not because I am the poster child for perfection and morality, but because the opposite is true. I am just as susceptible to a hard fall as anyone who has gone before me.

That is why I want to build guardrails into my life; Mark Beeson, my good friend, calls them "rumble strips."[1] Those are the bumpy grooves on the shoulder of a road that keep you from going into the ditch. Without rumble strips, you could be in the ditch before you know it.

No one is going to put rumble strips in your life for you. That is up to you. Your rumble strips may not be the same as mine, and mine may not be the same as yours. But everyone needs rumble strips. It all begins with self-leadership; before we talk about leading a church or a business, we must talk about being a leader worth following.

CHAPTER ONE

LIVE A LIFE WITH MARGINS

A MARGIN IS THE PORTION OF THE PAGE THAT YOU intentionally leave blank. You will notice on this page that the printers didn't put text all the way from the left side of the page to the right side. Rather, they left space all the way around—those are *margins*.

Yet in life, everything in our culture is telling us to ignore margins. Spend more money than you make, and you will have no financial margin. Fill your schedule from early morning until late night, and you will have no time margin. Surround yourself with needy people and constantly be reactive to their expectations, and you will have no emotional margin.

Mark Batterson wrote, "You need margin to *think*. You need margin to *play*. You need margin to *laugh*. You need margin to *dream*. You need margin to have *impromptu conversations*. You need margin to seize *unanticipated opportunities*."[1]

I want to live a life with margins.

When I live on less than I make, I have the financial margin so an unexpected expense won't capsize me, and so I can respond in the moment to someone else's real need.

When every moment of my life is scheduled, I don't have the margin to stop and listen to someone who needs an ear; I don't have the time to jump in and help a neighbor fix his sprinkler; I don't have the flexibility to go to one of my kids' sporting events that was scheduled at the last minute.

Margin makes you pleasant; no margin makes you grumpy.

Margin allows you to be generous; no margin makes you Scrooge-like.

Margin helps you listen. Without margin, you come across as someone who doesn't care.

Margin gives you the space to learn, grow, and dream. Without margin you become stale and empty.

Most important, margin increases the chance you will hear the still, small voice of God when he speaks. Without margin, you might continue through life without the blessing of God.

And yet I think it is safe to say that most leaders in America live without margin. We don't want to live that way, but we find ourselves constantly trying to catch our breaths.

Here are some practical ideas on how to create margin:

- Carve time into your week for margin. I liked to stack all my meetings on two days each week, which gave me margin to be responsive on the other days.
- Live on 80 percent of your income. Set aside another 10 percent for regular designated giving (church, charity, and more). Put the final 10 percent in a separate account to respond to whatever God might prompt your heart toward.
- Know yourself. What drains you emotionally? What fills your emotional tank? Be sure to schedule time to refill your tank with activities that add life to you. (More on this in chapter 4.)

- Minimize the number of life-sucking people around you. It's okay to have some relationships where you give 200 percent and they give nothing, but if all your relationships are like that, you'll die a slow, lonely death.
- Every now and then turn off the noise. You can't hear from God if you are constantly listening to the beep of the newest e-mail, the vibration of the latest text, the alert from your Twitter feed, or the chirp of a new Facebook notification. Schedule an electronic detox on occasion, and take time to listen to God, others, and yourself. This is so crucial I'm devoting chapter 3 to it.

THINK ABOUT IT

1. Where are you feeling the lack of margin in your life?

2. If you made just one change to increase margin in your life, what would that be?

CHAPTER TWO

WHEREVER YOU ARE,
BE FULLY THERE

TEENS GET A LOT OF GRIEF ABOUT HOW MUCH TIME THEY spend on their phones. I hear adults say, "They never put their phones down!" or "He is texting nonstop!" or "I bet she couldn't live a day without her phone." But in truth, teens do what teens see. And I see adults every day who belittle others because of the bad phone habits that they, too, model.

One day a couple of years ago I got up before daylight and spent hours traveling by plane to go across the country for the sole purpose of a one-hour meeting with some leaders for whom I have huge respect. I had looked forward to this meeting for weeks, waiting to hear their stories and grateful for the opportunity to share what God was doing through our partnership.

During the meeting, there were several points at which each of those leaders picked up his phone to read or type. At the same time, they glanced up at me on occasion as I was talking, said, "Uh-huh," then continued to "thumble" with their phones. I don't think I'd be exaggerating to say it was a rare moment in that one-hour meeting when one of them wasn't looking at or typing on his phone. I'm not a touchy-feely type of guy, but on that day I felt devalued. I felt as if there was something they would rather be doing, but they just didn't have the guts to tell me that this meeting was not a priority. I walked away from that meeting determined never to do that to anyone.

Here are a few "fully there" habits I appreciate in others and try to put in to practice myself:

- When you start a meeting, turn off your ringer and move the phone away from you. If the screen comes to life when you get a text, then turn the phone upside down so you won't see it. If it is likely to vibrate, then put it somewhere it can't be felt or heard.
- If your phone does vibrate during the meeting and your guest says, "Go ahead and answer it," reach down and silence it without even looking. This communicates to your guest that he or she is very valuable to you.
- Don't buy in to the "What if there is an emergency?" line. Rarely does that happen. It is not a good excuse for looking at your phone multiple times during every meeting.
- If you know you will need to be reached during the meeting, let your guest know, "My wife is at the doctor's office and may need to reach me, so I apologize in advance that I'll be taking her call when it comes." That tells your guest this is an exception—you wouldn't normally do this.
- If you are in a meeting with multiple people, follow the same rules. Don't convince yourself that your participation isn't needed so you can disengage and respond to texts or play Candy Crush Saga. We fool ourselves into thinking we can multitask, or that our disengagement won't be noticed for a few minutes. Not true.

I'm not saying phones are evil or that every time you use your phone you are devaluing others. I'm a heavy smartphone user. Your phone doesn't need to be out of sight every time you interact with another human. There are times when I'm sitting around with five or six friends or family members and every one of us has a phone out. That's part of the twenty-first century. I even think it can enhance the conversation and social interaction. But there are times when you have limited interaction with others and you should be *all* there.

It's about valuing people. And sometimes that means we are looking in someone's eyes and being fully engaged so we can really listen to the person's story and hear his or her heart.

THINK ABOUT IT

1. What habit do you need to change so people know you are fully listening to them?

2. If you are really brave, ask your spouse if he (or she) believes you are fully present when he (or she) is talking to you. Ask your coworkers. What do they say?

CHAPTER THREE

GO DARK

I HAVE A CONFESSION. I WAS ADDICTED TO THE TELEVISION show *24*. I watched every week and couldn't wait for Jack Bauer to save the world, once more, from some terrifying attack that was going to kill millions of people. And he always came through, just as the seconds ticked down.

Occasionally Jack would go deep undercover. No one could reach him. There was no way for anyone to communicate with him to change or abort the mission. Once he went dark, he would stay under until the mission was accomplished.

If you remove the intensity, gunfire, adrenaline-racing action, occasional psychotic behavior, and torture, then I think there are some real-life lessons we can learn from Jack Bauer. Sometimes we also need to go dark.

Most of the time you are available. People know where your office is. They know your e-mail address. They know how to reach you on Facebook or Twitter. They probably even have your cell-phone number. Perhaps they can connect with you through Xbox, Instagram, Tumblr, or a thousand additional ways that are being thought up as I write.

And there is nothing wrong with being connected in our fast-paced world. But there are times when you must intentionally disconnect. Maybe you do this by turning off your phone and iPad at eight every night and leaving it off until the next morning. Maybe you do this by disconnecting from everything one day each week.

So what exactly does *going dark* mean in today's world?

The Urban Dictionary website defines it this way: "To disappear; to become suddenly unavailable or digitally out of reach for an undefined period of time."[1]

For me, this usually means the following:

- I don't check e-mail.
- I make sure my e-mails stop forwarding to my phone.
- I don't carry my cell phone.
- I don't check any office voice mails.
- I don't blog. I also don't read anyone else's blogs.
- I don't tweet or go on Facebook (except for family stuff or pictures about my week).
- I don't read how-to-be-a-better-leader books (like this one).
- If I'm still in town, I don't stop by the office. I also don't go to my church.

I don't wait to go dark only when I'm on vacation or out of town. Instead, I plan this in advance because I know it's important. It is what I must do for my health and sanity, and for the wellness of my soul. I don't wait until I'm desperate—by then it's probably too late.

Last year I planned well in advance, and by the time my going-dark week arrived, I was on the edge. A good friend looked at me and said, "The life has drained out of your face." It had been an intense season and a long haul without much of a break. It was time to disconnect.

I've been asked, "Don't you miss a lot of important stuff when you go dark?" Yep. When I choose to go dark, it means I miss some opportunities. I am not involved in some key decisions. I miss some calls and e-mails that were important. I miss some deadlines. I disappoint some people. And for an entire week, I am unavailable to my team.

But it also means that I'm back the following week in a better frame of mind to serve and lead. I have a brighter outlook for the future and more margin in my life.

I haven't mastered a healthy life of balanced living. But I think it is worth asking yourself some questions:

- Do you have someone in your life who can look you in the eyes and say, "Dude, you need a break!"?
- Do you realize that you can't wait for someone else to tell you to take a break? You are responsible for your health—no one else. It's great when you work in a place that also values your health, but ultimately you are responsible.
- Do you know what fills your tank emotionally, physically, and spiritually? For me, when I spent fifty hours in one week last year engineering, hammering, drilling, sawing, and measuring, it brought amazing healing and health. And doing it with my dad, being surrounded by my kids and wife, and having my mom around, those relationships added to the joy. (More on this in the next chapter.)

You can't wait to take a break until the work is done or until no one else needs you. Those days will likely never come. It's possible that the best thing you can do is disappoint someone in the short run so that you can serve him or her better in the long run.

THINK ABOUT IT

1. When is the last time you disconnected digitally in order to renew your body, soul, or mind?

2. Consider taking time right now to put your go-dark week on the calendar.

CHAPTER FOUR

KNOW YOURSELF

MY WIFE AND I OFTEN GET A LAUGH OUT OF HOW DIFFER-
ent we are from each other. She lives for parties—in fact, the longer
she is at a party, bouncing around talking to people and laughing,
the more energetic she becomes. On the other hand, if you watch
me at a party, it would be similar to watching a balloon lose all
its air—minus the bouncing around the room part. My energy is
sucked away when I'm in large gatherings of people, especially if I
don't know them well.

I think the best marriages are made when two people understand what fills the tank of their spouse, and when they each do
everything they can to make sure it stays filled. And I think the
best leaders know what gives them energy, and they know what
drains it away.

I'm in my forties, and I'm just now beginning to figure myself
out. I'm realizing that to be whole and healthy, there are certain
things I need:

- I need to give. A lifestyle of generosity keeps me focused on
  others more than myself.
- I need to know I'm succeeding. When I don't know if I'm

doing the right things or doing them well enough, I begin to feel off balance.

- I need to design and build. If there is an alternate universe, I'm pretty sure I'm an architect over there. I love to dabble in engineering or designing, and then to build or manage the project to completion. Sometimes this might be a deck, other times it might be an organizational change, or occasionally it will be a multimillion-dollar building project.

- I need quiet time. I'm not a person who prays on my knees for a specific amount of time each day. I try to whisper prayers to God and listen to his voice all day long. Quiet time in the car, in my office, or at home helps me do this.

- I need eight to nine hours of sleep a night, and every now and then a good twelve-hour night. I envy people who can live on less sleep, but that ain't me.

- I need quality time with my kids. When they were younger, I spent time with them because they needed it. As they get older, I gain as much by my time with them as they do. They challenge me, inspire me, and make me laugh.

- I need a few friends: people who let me be me, who understand my quirks, who laugh *with* me (not *at* me), and who know I'm not mad when I'm quiet.

- I need to write. Writing is a passion. When I can't find the time to write, I feel mentally constipated. When I have time to write, everything in my brain flows more freely. (Probably not the best analogy, but I'm guessing you know what I mean.)

It is my guess that your list is much different from mine. Perhaps you love food and need to prepare or enjoy an amazing meal on occasion. Maybe you regain energy by spending regular time in nature. Perhaps it is music that refills your tank. Or maybe you need to start something new from scratch and watch it soar.

You won't always get what you need. No one does. There are many seasons when I have to ask God for grace to get through a period of too little rest or too much work. But when I'm feeling stressed or tense, it's often because I'm not paying attention to my list.

You might feel like this exercise is a bit self-focused. Maybe it is, but I believe God has wired each of us uniquely, and we have to know what we need if we are going to lead others effectively. To be the person I need to be for my kids, my wife, my job, and my friends, there are certain things I need.

It is important to figure out what it is that you really need to be the person God wants you to be. Some of this is learned over time and from experience, but you can also make a list with the help of friends and family who know you best.

If you are going to lead others with strength, then you must lead from a place of strength—and that requires knowing yourself.

THINK ABOUT IT

1. Do you know what you need to be whole, loving, and full of grace? What is it?

2. Make a list of things you need and share it with your spouse or a close friend. See if there is anything that surprises that person, and talk about how you can integrate your list more fully into your life.

CHAPTER FIVE

STAY HOME FROM CHURCH

MANY YEARS AGO ONE OF THE PASTORS AT THE CHURCH where I worked decided to take a staycation for a week to get some stuff done around his house. On Sunday morning, he showed up at church in jeans and a T-shirt (which wouldn't be too abnormal now, but back in the early nineties it was strange). I was standing nearby when a volunteer asked him a question, and he responded, "You'll need to call me next week, I'm on vacation."

Was he serious? You can't go to your own church and pretend to be on vacation. That would be like a restaurant owner going to dinner at her own restaurant and refusing to answer questions or solve problems because it was her day off.

There is an added layer of complexity and tension for those who work at a church. As a pastor or church leader, you do everything you can to offer great environments and experiences for people to meet God on Sunday. But there is a reality that sometimes going to church is not what *you* need to take *your* next spiritual step. In fact, sometimes going to church might even damage your soul.

Let me break it down.

Place Doesn't Matter

- God does not live at your church. (I hear gasps of disbelief.) It's true. Some of the most unspiritual people I've met are those who spend the greatest amounts of time at church. They attend every Bible study and every prayer gathering, and sign up for every event and team, but still they manage to avoid becoming godly, or even nice to be around. If you had to choose between cutting off your leg and spending more time with those people—be honest—it would take a few minutes to decide.
- A pastor's job is not to create automatons who come every time the church doors are open. He or she helps people grow in their love for God and their love for others. Most times that happens best away from the church property.
- Church attendance and involvement are poor substitutes for genuine spiritual health.

Pay Attention to Your Indicators

- If you are sitting in your own church service but find your mind wandering to the things that need to be fixed, the people who need to be corrected, or the systems that need to be added—instead of learning or worshiping—that's probably a sign that you need to get away.
- You have to know what fills your spiritual and emotional tanks. Sometimes that might be singing worship songs with hundreds of people. Other times it might be riding a motorcycle, reading a book, or playing a video game.
- I can tell when I'm feeling "fried." If I keep up the same pace, I'm going to lose my love for my job and will begin to

lose effectiveness. When I begin to feel toasty, I need to get away.

- Sometimes sleep is the most spiritual thing you can do.

Healthy Separation Is Okay

- Don't worry about what people will think of you if you skip a service. You don't have to advertise it, but if someone asks, use it as an opportunity to let the person know you are focused on your spiritual health, and that's why you stayed home from church.
- When church leaders begin to see their people become less involved in the activity of the church, it doesn't necessarily mean they are backsliding or falling away from God. It might mean they actually get it now, and they are practicing the Jesus-life where it matters: in their relationships and communities.

I love my church. I can't imagine a more effective place for followers of Christ to grow or for the unconvinced to explore their questions. I don't know of a place that has better artistic elements that soften my heart and open my mind. I've never been to a church that has a more dynamic teaching team to communicate the gospel. I gave my life full-time for two decades to my church. And yet, every now and then, the most spiritual thing I could do was stay away!

THINK ABOUT IT

1. For those who lead in church: Do you encourage your staff members to stay away from church on occasion for the sake of their spiritual health? If not, why don't you?

2. Do you feel guilty when you don't go to church? What does that reveal about what you think about God and his acceptance of you?

CHAPTER SIX

LEAVE A LEGACY

IT SEEMS AS IF EVERY WEEK OR SO I HEAR ABOUT PEOPLE who failed, recovered, and then wrote a book about it. Perhaps their marriages failed. Or they went through a phase as an addict. Or they lost their families because of bad choices. And so they write a book because of the insights they gained along the way.

I understand why those books sell. As fallen humans, we identify with other people who talk about their failures in such stark terms. We figure the author has some insight into the human condition, and perhaps we can learn enough to keep ourselves from falling in the same hole. And I agree; we can definitely learn from such people.

I recall more than twenty years ago when Gordon MacDonald went through a tough time. The guy who had written *Ordering Your Private World* saw his world publicly crash to the ground.[1] He later reflected on his fall and quoted Oswald Chambers with a phrase I'll never forget: "An unguarded strength is a double weakness."[2] He was saying, "Pay attention! I screwed up in an area where I was strong. Don't do the same."

So, yes, those who have fallen and recovered to some level of health have a place to write books and give talks about the pitfalls that should be avoided.

But what about those who were faithful for a lifetime, who never had a public failure, who loved their spouses for decades, who led their families with integrity, who ran businesses that cared for people as much as the bottom line? Why don't *they* write books? *Probably because no one would buy them.* The topic isn't as sexy, is it? You aren't going to hear much dirt or experience the highs and lows of a huge fall.

But I have to ask:

- Would you rather get advice from the man who messed up and lost his marriage or the man who has stood by his wife through ups and downs for thirty or forty years?
- Would you like to get parenting advice from authors who tell you all the mistakes they made and how they regret that they traveled so much and didn't spend time with their kids? Or would you rather hear from parents who were present, day in and day out, loving on and listening to their kids and now have young adult children who are grounded and secure?
- Would you rather get advice from the speaker who talks about all the bad things she did in her "wild, youthful days," including illegal substances and multiple sexual partners, or from the "boring" girl who studied during college, got married as a virgin, and stayed connected to God and her family?

The answer is not either/or. We can learn from both. I wish there were a way to identify and learn from the people who stay faithful day after day, year after year—but they don't tend to write books about their successes. It's possible their humility is one of the reasons for their stability.

Our entire culture is shaped to love a redemption story. The best movies are about people who went all the way to the bottom and then were rescued and ended up becoming heroes. And God specializes in redemption! It is in his nature to love a good redemption story.

I think we make a mistake, though, when we don't realize that every story is a redemption story (Rom. 3:10). On our own, we could never find our way to God. He reaches down and rescues us from our broken ways—and from ourselves—and sets us on a new path.

Those who are most aware of their humanity and their sinful nature are the ones who consistently make good choices in their lives and in their relationships. I want to hear more of those stories.

I challenge you to be a leader who walks with integrity day after day, year after year, decade after decade. What if you could go to your grave with no regrets about your relationship with your spouse, your commitment to your friends, the way you ran your business, or how you raised your children?

Every choice you make today will lead you either toward the path less traveled where you die with your integrity intact or toward a life of regrets. It's your choice.

THINK ABOUT IT

1. Who do you know who has consistently made good choices? Seek him or her out and ask questions. You might actually learn something.

2. What changes do you need to make right now so you will get to the end of your life with a legacy of integrity?

CHAPTER SEVEN

BE A LIFELONG LEARNER

WHEN I WAS NINETEEN YEARS OLD, I WAS TRYING TO DECIDE if I should go to college. I had been out of high school for two years, working in the real world in a leadership environment. A management consultant came to town and spent several days assessing our leadership team. I asked him to spend some time helping me determine whether I should continue on my current path or go to college.

I'll never forget the advice I received: "College is a great environment for three groups of people: (a) those who need structure to learn, (b) those who are trying to figure out what they want to do with their lives, or (c) those who need a degree to pursue their goals."

Then he said, "Tim, you don't fit any of those categories. You have proven that you are wired as a learner, and you don't need college to keep learning."

And I've been on a path of lifelong learning ever since. As far as I know, I've never been denied any opportunities because I don't have a college degree. If you narrowly define learning and education by how long an individual spent in a classroom setting, then you greatly misunderstand learning.

One of the biggest differences between leaders and followers is that leaders are learners.

John Maxwell put it this way:

> In a study of ninety top leaders from a variety of fields, leadership expert Warren Bennis and Burt Nanus made a discovery about the relationship between growth and leadership: "It is the capacity to develop and improve their skills that distinguish leaders from their followers." Successful leaders are learners. And the learning process is ongoing, a result of self-discipline and perseverance. The goal each day must be to get a little better, to build on the previous day's progress.[1]

You have to decide how you learn best. It might be books for some, conferences or hands-on environments for others.

I find that some of my greatest learning experiences have been when I've had the chance to gather with a small group of leaders for the sole purpose of sharing ideas, brainstorming, considering the future, and talking about trends. Think less conference and more round table. This is more about coaching than workshops or seminars.

You might be the type of learner who sits and soaks. I think best when I can take notes. At a recent gathering, the facilitator asked us to put our laptops and papers away for the workshop, and it nearly disabled me. He assumed his learning style would help us all. He was wrong. There is no right way to learn.

I have a close friend who loves to debate concepts and theories. He learns tremendously from those conversations. I'm a practitioner. I don't do theory well for very long. At some point, it's got to make sense. It must answer the question, what the heck does this mean in the real world?

Some learners require a teacher. Others require structure. Some can't learn unless they are alone. I am a research fanatic. Smartphones and iPads were made for guys like me who love constantly and instantly to be learning more about the things they see or people they meet.

Business leaders are beginning to learn more from church leaders; one of the largest leadership conferences in the world, attended by thousands of business leaders, is hosted by Willow Creek Community Church.[2] Likewise, church leaders have so much they can learn from business leaders. I get some tremendous ideas from *Fast Company* and *Wired* magazines. For example, recently I read this about Toyota:

> If your factory is just making cars, once a day the whistle blows and it's quitting time, no more cars to make that day. If your factory is making a new way to make cars, the whistle never blows, you're never done.[3]

Here is how I translated it for the church: If your church is just about putting on great weekend services, every Sunday at noon the whistle blows and it's quitting time, no more services. You can put a big, fat check mark in the box because you pulled it off. However, if your church is about making disciples who reproduce and make more disciples, the whistle never blows—you're never done.

Be a lifelong learner, always looking for what God is teaching you, and one sentence from a business magazine could change the way your church or business is organized.

THINK ABOUT IT

1. How do you learn best? Are you making sure your schedule allows time to learn?

2. If you aren't naturally wired as a learner, what can you build into your regular routine that will enhance learning opportunities?

CHAPTER EIGHT

GET NAKED

I WAS SITTING IN A WEEKLY STAFF MEETING RECENTLY, AND Kem Meyer, one of my good friends and a coleader on Granger's executive team, was leading. She is a wonderful mom and was telling a story of being at the beach a few days prior with her friend. They each had their twelve-year-old boys with them, and the kids eventually wandered out a couple hundred feet into Lake Michigan. That wouldn't be a bad thing on a normal day, but what she didn't realize was that there were rip current warnings all up and down the shore. It was dangerous to be in the water that day.

Kem recounted the helpless feeling of watching her son and his friend struggling for their lives, arms waving, going under the water again and again only to resurface gasping for air. There was nothing she could do—the current was too strong for her and the other mom.

The staff was completely silent as she told about another man nearby who swam in and rescued the boys. You would think the story was about the miracle of this hero. And that was part of it. But the notable part of the story was Kem's humility as she talked about how she failed as a mom, and how that failure almost cost the life of her son.

I sat there trying to figure out how it was that a leader talking about a failure made me respect her more, not less. She said, "I messed up," and yet almost every person in the room wanted to follow her more than before she told the story.

When I was younger, I was more interested in image management. It seemed as though there was a certain expectation for how I should act, what I should say, where I should go, and even what I should think.

Sometimes my thoughts would scare me. I believed if people knew about my doubts or fears, I would lose their respect. If anyone knew that I didn't have the answers to the questions in my mind, I might lose my standing.

I don't know if I changed or my surroundings changed, but I now believe almost the exact opposite. I think the most attractive leaders are those who reveal that they don't know everything.

Patrick Lencioni is a great author and speaker. In a talk at the 2011 Global Leadership Summit, he gave several principles from his book *Getting Naked*.[1] I found much of what he said to be quite insightful:

- People don't embrace vulnerability because it runs counter to our need to protect ourselves from suffering.
- We think we can't be vulnerable because of our fear of losing business.
- When we are serving others, we have to do things and ask questions that might embarrass ourselves.
- My job isn't to look smart; it is to help people do better.
- When we acknowledge our humanity, it attracts people. They want to be around us.[2]

There is a fine line, however, between being selectively vulnerable and vomiting your problems to anyone at any time. One is attractive. The other repels. One is the sign of a great leader. The other is the sign of a person in need of therapy.

Here are some thoughts that might help you take steps toward being vulnerable:

- Don't be manipulatively vulnerable. In other words, don't be vulnerable in order to get something out of the person (or crowd) you are talking to. People will see right through your facade.
- Your vulnerability should increase with those in your closest circle. You shouldn't give as many details to a crowd of strangers as you would to your closest friends.
- Vulnerability and trust are dependent on each other. It's tough to be vulnerable outside the context of a trusting relationship. However, it's also tough to build trust if you aren't willing to be vulnerable. Thus, there is a little bit of risk involved in choosing to be vulnerable.
- There is one easy way to begin practicing vulnerability: The next time you are asked a question and don't know the answer, admit it. Just say, "I have no idea."

Another word for "vulnerable" is *humble*. In James 4:6, we are told, "God opposes the proud, but gives grace to the humble" (ESV). I think the same may be true of the people around us. When we choose the path of pride rather than humility, we keep people at arm's length.

Three years ago I told my Granger senior team, with tears in my eyes, "I have to drive down to see Heather [my daughter] at her college tomorrow and tell her that her youth pastor has disqualified himself from ministry, and then I have to tell her that her uncle is dying. And I have no idea how to do that." A few months later one of my friends who was present at that meeting told me her respect for me went up that day since I went to a new level of vulnerability with the group.

It's okay to admit you are human. In fact, the leaders for whom I have the greatest respect are often the most vulnerable.

THINK ABOUT IT

1. Would the people around you say that you are a vulnerable leader?

2. Have there been times when you've cared more about looking smart and having the right answers than being a trusted leader? If so, what can you do about it?

CHAPTER NINE

CONTROL YOUR CALENDAR

MARK BATTERSON WROTE, "IF YOU DON'T CONTROL YOUR calendar, your calendar will control you."[1]

Alan Lakein said, "Time is life. It is irreversible and irreplaceable. To waste your time is to waste your life, but to master your time is to master your life and make the most of it."[2]

M. Scott Peck is credited with saying, "Until you value yourself, you will not value your time. Until you value your time, you will not do anything with it."[3]

And I've heard a hundred preachers say, "Show me your checkbook and your calendar, and I'll tell you what you value."

I agree with all these statements. Leaders who don't have control of their calendars will constantly be spinning out in the dirt without making much progress. Life will seem frantic and harried, yet it will be difficult to pinpoint what they are actually getting done.

I'm not the king of time management, but I do live and die by my calendar. Everything that is important in my life goes on my calendar. Here are six principles that help me:

1. Put priority items on your calendar first. Perhaps you've seen the illustration where the presenter tries to fill a jar with a

combination of big rocks and little rocks. If the presenter fills the jar with the little rocks first, he is not able to fit very many big rocks in the jar. However, if he fills it with all the big rocks first, then he can add many of the little rocks around the big rocks. The analogy breaks down if you go very far with it, but the foundation is true. You must put priority things (e.g., time with your spouse and kids, vacation, strategic planning, and vision time) on the calendar first. Otherwise you'll never find time for those priorities.

2. Stack your meetings. If it's within your control, try to schedule all your meetings on the same day or two each week. I knew I wouldn't get much productive work done on those days, but I was going to have some great conversations, help move the ball down the field on some projects, and keep my staff moving forward because of our connections. Stacking your meetings will keep you from getting bitter about meetings ruling your life, and it will leave you with a couple of days where your schedule is relatively open.

3. Schedule your rest. If you don't plan for rest and renewal, it won't happen. My calendar will always fill up if I don't plan for some down time. I'm always amazed when I hear people say, "I'm going to try to take a couple of days off next week. I just have to see how the week goes." *What? Are you kidding?* You can't wait for the right time to unwind or take a vacation with your family. It will never happen. Get the dates on the calendar months in advance. Always be looking at your schedule for busy seasons ahead. Make sure you plan some time in the middle of those seasons to unwind and get centered.

4. Manage your travel schedule. If you don't travel, skip over this one. But many leaders have to be on the road. A few years ago I noticed my travel schedule was getting out of hand. One year I was gone eighteen nights, the next year

it was twenty-five, then thirty-two, then forty-seven. This was not a good trend. Because my kids were younger, and because my wife was not able to travel with me often, I was unwilling to see that trend continue. So I sat down with my wife and my boss, and we figured out that thirty nights away from home was a reasonable number for me during that season. Any more than that, and my priorities started to get out of whack. If it was much less than that, it was more difficult for me to get my job done. I don't think the number thirty is magical, but I do think it's important for anyone who travels regularly to find the right amount that balances family, business, and personal health.

5. Go home before the work is done. This is difficult whether you are in business or the church world. (In ministry, we convince ourselves someone might go to hell if we go home too soon!) When you go home before the work is done, it means you are leaving something really good behind. But you can't wait until your to-do list is complete or until the phone stops ringing before you head home to your family. The work is never finished. Just go home! (Note: If you are a slacker, then please ignore this point. You actually shouldn't leave until your to-do list is done.)

6. Leave room for people and leave room for God. It is easy to fill up your calendar and not leave room for what God might bring along your path. I had a friend who called these "God-a-dents" instead of accidents. If my calendar is booked solid, I don't have the flexibility when someone drops by my office or a crisis comes up that needs attention. I try to monitor this by blocking more time than is needed for appointments, leaving a buffer between appointments, and keeping my door open as often as possible. This is just as important for Christian business leaders. Part of your calling as a follower

of Jesus is to love and care for people—and that begins with the people already in your life. Make room to ask your employees about their lives, their dreams, and their hurts.

John Maxwell summed up calendar management this way: "The key to becoming a more efficient leader isn't checking off all the items on your to-do list each day. It's in forming the habit of prioritizing your time so that you are accomplishing your most important goals in an efficient manner."[4]

THINK ABOUT IT

1. What can you do right now to make sure your priorities get put on your calendar for the next six months?

2. Are you traveling too much? Consider sitting down with your spouse and boss and talking through some manageable parameters.

CHAPTER TEN

GUARD YOUR FAMILY

WHEN I WAS IN MY TWENTIES, I WAS MARRIED, WE DIDN'T have any kids, and my wife, Faith, and I chased each other around the house like rabbits. Keeping family a priority was easy. I couldn't wait to get home each day to spend more time with the love of my life.

When I got into my thirties, life began to get busy. We had a baby, then another, then another . . . and another. Then they turned into toddlers, and the pressure increased both at home and on the job. I loved my job and my family, so I tried to play it fifty-fifty. I tried to give both my best. But it started to be too much pressure.

A few years ago I went through a season where I thought I might lose my ministry. I thought there might be a time when I would no longer have my job and would lose my identity. I began thinking, *What would be left?* And I made the very intentional decision to no longer divide my focus fifty-fifty between my job and my home. I was going to make my family the priority.

Andy Stanley calls this "choosing to cheat" in his book by the same title.[1] He says we should cheat our jobs instead of cheating our families. I understand what he means, but I don't think I'm cheating my employer when I place the priority on my family.[2] I think it is exactly what my employer expects of me.

I heard Andy say to a group of guys, "We were never commanded to love the church. We were commanded to love our wives."[3] So true.

In June 2011, I spent a week with a consultant working on my life plan. I considered what my next phase of life should be about. We walked through my history, dreams, passions, opportunities, and more. It was an exhaustive process that helped me gain perspective and focus on the few things that should be central to my life. It should be no surprise that my next season revolved centrally around my family.

This doesn't just happen, though. It takes intentionality and advance planning. Here are a few practical ideas:

- Date nights. Dating is fun before you're married, it is natural when you are newlyweds, but it gets difficult when the babies start coming. New parents are nervous about leaving their kids with someone else; then a few years later it's hard to find money for childcare; later it's difficult enough juggling the kids' crazy schedules with sports and school activities. I know it is a pain, but it is crucial that you have a regular routine of spending time alone with your spouse. This communicates to each other, and to your kids, how you value your relationship.
- Walks together. My wife and I recently started a routine of walking together in the evenings. This gives us both a time to unwind, leave the kids behind, and spend thirty or forty minutes hearing about the other's day. I realize this is more difficult if your kids are smaller. Be creative; perhaps trade off with neighbors who have the same priority.
- One-on-one time with each kid. We have four children,

so trust me when I say this is very hard. In a good month I'd probably give myself a C plus. To be effective at this, you have to know what communicates love to your kids. My boys are not athletic. If I took them out to play catch, they would run and duck, wondering why I was throwing something at them. For one child it might be playing video games; for a daughter it might be dressing up for a date night; for another it might be going to a concert or event. Do intentional things so they know they are more important to you than your job. I heard Bill and Lynne Hybels say recently, "We knew when we started a church we were going to disappoint people. We just decided that we were never going to let it be our kids who were disappointed."[4]

- Yearly trips (no kids allowed). I'm going to say more about this later, but for now let me just say this will never be easy and it will likely not always make sense. But your regular trips give your kids a security that mommy and daddy love each other. They will face scores of friends from broken homes, so you need to go overboard to assure them that your love is strong.

- Check the thermostat. Men, this is especially for you. Your wife may be a better thermostat about your relationship than you are. I don't know how many times my wife has said, "How do you think we are doing?" and in my heart of hearts, I think we are doing great. I'm sure it's never been better. Then I hear her talk, and she reveals some areas where we could improve. In those moments, I can choose either to listen or to justify. I'm not saying she is infallible, but I do need to listen to her and stay tuned in to her sense of how the family is doing.

No one gets to the end of his or her life and says, "I wish I had spent more time at my job." But often you will hear people reflecting on poor choices with their families: "I wish I had been around more when the kids were little," or "We invested all our energy on the kids, and then when they left home there was nothing remaining for our relationship with each other."

For those of you who work in ministry, it can mess with your mind because you think that eternity is at stake and people's lives are on the line. "If I stay at the office just a little bit longer, I can help scores of people . . ." Yeah, and if you wreck your marriage or lose your family, you will damage hundreds of people. Don't let the lies of Satan lead you to have a mistress called "ministry" who gets more attention than your family.

THINK ABOUT IT

1. What are you intentionally doing to make sure your family is a higher priority than your job? What more can you do?

2. Look at your calendar. Does it reflect the priority you place on your spouse and kids? What could change?

CHAPTER ELEVEN

LEAVE YOUR KIDS BEHIND

I HAVE TO ASK A QUESTION. MOM, DO YOUR KIDS KNOW that your husband is the most important person in your life? Listen, Dad, do your kids see you prioritizing your wife regularly and deliberately above them?

Your kids will not feel this if you do not intentionally make the effort to reinforce it in your regular family life.

I believe one of the best ways to do this is to take a vacation together, every year, without the kids. We have figured out a way to do this every year for twenty-four years straight. And no, it's not easy. There are things like nursing and pregnancies you have to work around. (Trust me, I know. Faith was pregnant or nursing for six and a half years of our married life!) There are also real difficulties like money and childcare.

But you must do it. Here are three reasons I believe your marriage can't thrive without an annual kidless vacation:

1. Life is crazy! Regardless of how disciplined you are with daily or weekly time together with your wife, life gets busy and stressed, and you need some extended time to reconnect with your spouse to get grounded again in each other's love.

2. Your kids won't always be around. If you are not spending time together to develop your marriage relationship, one day, when the kids are gone, you will find you have nothing in common.

3. Your kids need to see you making this relationship a priority. If they don't see a healthy marriage at home, where will they see it?

I hear all kinds of excuses for not planning a no-kids-allowed vacation:

- DON'T BLAME IT ON MONEY. There are cheap ways to vacation. In our first few years of marriage (when our income put us right at the official poverty level), we committed to time away and left it in God's hands. More than once, someone came along and said, "Hey, we have a cabin you can use if you want," and we had a great vacation for the cost of getting there. Pray for provision, and keep your eye out for less expensive alternatives like camping or staying with friends.

- DON'T BLAME IT ON TIME. You'll never have enough time for it to make sense. Decide what is important to you (answer: your marriage!), and get it on the schedule.

- DON'T BLAME IT ON THE KIDS. The greatest way to show your kids how valuable they are to you is to take time for each other. Work with another couple who is also committed to time away, and watch each other's kids. Ask grandparents to step in and help, and don't worry about how spoiled they will get in your absence. It only takes a few days to get everything back in line and on schedule.

- DON'T BLAME IT ON YOUR JOB. Are you still waiting until the work slows down? Or until you finish the big project? Or until you get the promotion and have more vacation days available? Wait long enough, and you might have a great job and no marriage. If you sincerely can't get time off work, then plan a couple extended weekends.

What does all this have to do with leadership? Everything! A leader who is successful at work but a failure at home is not a successful leader. The first test of leadership is your ability to love, lead, and care for those who are closest to you.

Here is the truth. You will likely have many years of marriage after your kids have all left home. If you don't work on your marriage during the parenting years, you might not have a relationship left as empty nesters. Be intentional.

THINK ABOUT IT

1. What are you doing to intentionally build your marriage in ways that will last well after your kids are gone?

2. Perhaps you've been thinking about planning time away with your spouse, but you just haven't pulled the trigger. Wait no longer. Schedule it now.

CHAPTER TWELVE

DEVELOP RUMBLE STRIPS

NEWS FLASH: *I AM A MAN.* THAT MAY HAVE CAUGHT SOME of you by surprise, but it is true. I am a man, and I work many hours every week with women. I spend a lot of time with some of them. In fact, some weeks I spend more time with my female coworkers than with my wife.

I think a work environment or ministry setting that includes both men and women has the potential to be incredibly healthy and effective. There is a unique perspective brought from both sexes that is incomplete when one or the other is missing. I've worked in some settings where it felt like a boys' club, and we were not everything we needed to be. Men need female leaders to be at the table, making decisions and defining direction with them.

But anytime there are heterosexual men and women in the same environment, there is the potential for sexual tension, wayward desires, and in the worst cases, inappropriate behavior. If that happens in most marketplace offices, apologies are made, people might be transferred, or occasionally someone gets fired. When it happens in the church, people are devastated, the mission is interrupted for a season, and scores of people are left questioning their faith.

The stakes are high for followers of Jesus, whether in business or in the church. That's why it is important to have some personal rumble strips in place. We talked about the concept of rumble strips or boundaries earlier—the kind you encounter on the side of the highway. When you hit rumble strips while you're driving, it doesn't mean you did anything wrong. But it does mean that if you continue on that path, you are going to go off the road and wreck your life.

Here are a few rumble strips we chose to live by at Granger:

- We never went out to eat alone with the opposite sex. Yes, this was a pain. There were times when a business lunch would have helped to move a project along. But we chose not to so others wouldn't draw a wrong conclusion, and so there would be no room for temptation. Many times we had food brought to the office if we needed to work through lunch.

- We never traveled alone with the opposite sex. Not even across town, and surely not out of town. I saw a female friend come to a conference with a male business associate, and after the meeting she left with her associate, walking together with him to the hotel their company had booked. Alarms started going off in my head. *Why would they do that? Isn't she concerned about the perception of their company? Doesn't this bother their spouses?* A few months later I learned that she was having an affair with a business partner. I was sad but not shocked.

  Yes, this makes it very inconvenient to travel. There were times when I needed to be in the same place as a female associate, and so we brought a third person along. That cost money and reduced productivity. But we didn't want to sidetrack the church with needless accusations.

- We never met in a closed room alone with the opposite sex. We actually designed every office in our building so there was a window to a hallway. There were times when a private conversation was necessary. In that case, the window blinds to the hallway were opened as the door was closed.

I've integrated a few additional rumble strips that are important to me personally:

- I don't become a sounding board for marital difficulties. If I have a female staff member who is struggling in her relationship with her husband, I am not going to be the best person to help her. Why? Because of my proximity to her. I want to be aware of what is going on in her life and with her kids, but I do not let it transition into "This is what I don't like about my husband," or "This is where my husband is not meeting my needs." At that point, she needs to be talking to a female friend or a counselor.
- It is important to me that the women I work with most closely are also friends with my wife. I don't want there ever to be a hint of mistrust from my wife about the women I work with. We try to find ways to hang out as couples, and I encourage my wife and my female coworkers to find ways to hang out together. I believe this offers an extra level of protection for our marriages.
- Someone always knows where I am. I freely and willingly use the Find My Friends app on my iPhone and iPad, and I never turn it off. There are currently sixteen people who can know my exact location at any moment in time. I think that is a healthy rumble strip, especially when I'm traveling alone. Before I leave, I will send an e-mail to my wife and two or three friends and tell them my exact schedule,

encourage them to track me on Find My Friends, and give them permission to call me at any time to make sure I'm actually with my phone. I do this for three reasons: (1) I don't want the potential for an unfounded accusation of what I did while I was out of town, (2) I'm not immune to stumbling, and (3) I want to give an extra level of security and confidence to my wife and close friends that I am staying focused and on task.

I don't share these rumble strips because I'm a saint. I share them because I'm not. I don't trust myself. I don't trust people who would love to see me fall and my family or the organization I am working for damaged. I don't want my actions to cause leaders at my organization to have to spend time and energy figuring out if I did something I was accused of.

It's not about rules for me. I do this because I love those I work with and for. And I love my wife. And I love the marriages of my close friends. For those reasons, I choose a few inconveniences.

THINK ABOUT IT

1. What rumble strips do you need to put in place for yourself?

2. What rumble strips should you consider having everyone on your staff or team agree to?

CHAPTER THIRTEEN

BE CAREFUL WHAT YOU WISH FOR

MY BACKYARD IS TO DIE FOR. ASK ANYONE WHO HAS SEEN it. It is more than an acre, with a huge playset, two tree houses connected by a bridge, a swimming pool, a zip line, a tire swing, trees to climb, plenty of room to run, and a huge forest to hide in and build forts.

I remember walking outside one summer day and finding a hideout the boys had built just over the fence. It was in another yard, belonging to someone we'd never met—and someone who had not given us permission to be in his yard.

With such a huge adventure available in our own yard, what would drive them to cross the fence? Why is it so enticing to be in someone else's yard? What is so tempting about the other side of the fence?

I think it has something to do with our flesh. No matter how wide the parameters or how broad the boundary markers, something in our makeup pulls us across the fence.

Another example: The tanning industry is strong in the United States. Women with darker skin captivate American men. That's not true in every country. I saw a travel show about Brazil recently.

A cab driver was being interviewed and talked about how Brazilian men are captivated by women with fair skin and blond hair. When asked the reason for this and told it was the opposite in the States, the cab driver astutely noted that people everywhere seem to want what they don't have.

He may not have known it, but his observation is straight out of the New Testament:

> Don't love the world's ways. Don't love the world's goods. Love of the world squeezes out love for the Father. Practically everything that goes on in the world—wanting your own way, wanting everything for yourself, wanting to appear important—has nothing to do with the Father. It just isolates you from him. The world and all its wanting, wanting, wanting is on the way out—but whoever does what God wants is set for eternity. (1 John 2:15–17 MSG)

Your marriage is great, but there is a relationship just across the fence that is interesting and exciting. You leave your wife at home in sweatpants with her hair messed up and the smell of baby diapers all over her, and you go to the office where the women look nice and smell sweet, and you ask, *Could life be better on the other side of the fence?*

You have enough money, but you think the amount of money just across the fence would make you happier or give you more freedom. Gallup recently did a poll that said those making less than $50,000 annually thought they would be rich and happy if they made $100,000. Those who were paid more than $50,000 thought it would take $200,000 or more to be happy. And those making more than $75,000 thought it would take $250,000.[1] We want what we don't have. Until we get it, and then we want more.

You're doing great watching your weight, but it sucks to have to count every calorie. That juicy cheeseburger just across the fence surely won't take you too far offtrack.

In your yard you are single; surely the married yard is better. Or you are married and wish you were single again. Or you don't have kids and wish you did. Or you have kids and can't wait until they are out of the house, like the couple across the fence who has total freedom with their time.

We live in a society that is geared to make you want what you don't have. We are exposed to as many as five thousand advertising messages every single day.[2] That number is increasing. And nearly every message's aim is to show you something you don't have but probably need.

This is a problem we will likely never conquer. It will be with us for all our lives. But here are some practices I think are good antidotes to keep the Want-Monster in check:

- Become a generous person. "One person gives freely, yet gains even more; another withholds unduly, but comes to poverty. A generous person will prosper" (Prov. 11:24–25). Generosity is the best antidote for selfishness and greed.
- Spend time with people who have less than you. Do what you can to lift others out of poverty. "Defend the rights of the poor and needy" (Prov. 31:9).
- Visit GlobalRichList.com and enter your annual income. You will quickly understand how blessed you are. For example, a person making $20,000 a year is in the top 4 percent of the richest people in the world.
- Work on developing your character. Start by focusing on the fruit of the Spirit found in Galatians 5:22–23.

Yes, there is something enticing about the possibilities across the fence. Don't beat yourself up for wanting stuff. That is human.

There is nothing sinful about the temptation. But begin to develop practices of how you will handle your desires when they begin to crowd out what is good and right.

THINK ABOUT IT

1. Have you crossed any fences in your marriage, family, or financial decisions? What will you do, right now, to move back toward Jesus?

2. Are your wants out of control? Which of these practices do you need to begin immediately to refocus on your faith and priorities?

PART TWO

FIND THE RIGHT PEOPLE

I'LL ADMIT TO BEING A BIT OF A POLITICAL JUNKIE, AND I especially get into it during election season. The constant speeches, commentaries, jockeying for the spotlight, sound bites, dramatic missteps, and political maneuvering fascinate me. And when somebody new wins, it's such a spectacle to watch as the victor moves into the White House and begins his first days in office.

There are about seventy-five days that pass between Election Day and Inauguration Day when the winning candidate will begin the new presidency. And every single day is filled with pundits and politicians guessing what will happen when the new leader of the free world finally takes his or her place in the Oval Office.

What will the president do during the next four years? What about in the first few days? Will the economy improve? Will he appoint conservatives or liberals on the Supreme Court? Will she focus on securing our borders? Will she fix health care or repair social security? Will he set policies to avert another recession?

Good questions. But I believe the biggest decisions the next president of the United States makes will happen during the transitional days before he or she arrives at 1600 Pennsylvania Avenue. Few people are paying attention, but the most significant leadership moves of the president's entire four- or eight-year presidential career will be made before the winner ever steps into the Oval Office.

That's because, more than any other decisions, the team presidents surround themselves with determines their success—and the strength of the nation. Bill Clinton chose people like Dick Morris and George Stephanopoulos; Ronald Reagan chose James Bakker and William Clark; George W. Bush worked with Karl Rove and Donald Rumsfeld. And President Obama selected Hillary Clinton and Timothy Geithner in his first term.

Here is what I believe to my core: the success of leaders will rise or fall based on the decisions they make about the people around them.

It is true for you as well. If you are a chief executive, a senior pastor, or a leader of a department or ministry, your greatest leadership challenge is surrounding yourself with the right people. It doesn't matter how good you are alone; if you don't have the right people around you, representing you and pulling with you, your leadership potential will eventually be capped.

Just as important as picking the right people is making the tough decision to release one when you've made a bad choice. I think that may have been one of George W. Bush's leadership weaknesses. He was so loyal to his picks that he proved to be unable to release them when it became apparent they could no longer lead because of incompetence or the political landscape.

I have been asked many times, "What is the most important thing you did as an executive pastor?" It's an easy answer: finding and releasing leaders. My job was to bring the right people on the team, give them the resources to do ministry well, and gracefully release them if necessary.

It is from that lens that I offer some highly practical chapters on finding the right people.

CHAPTER FOURTEEN

A RÉSUMÉ IS WORTHLESS

ONE DAY THE PHONE RANG AND IT WAS BILL, A FRIEND WHO was asking me if I'd take a look at his résumé. I say he is my friend because I know him and I'm friendly toward him. But because he is lazy, a constant complainer, and blows every little thing into a huge drama, I don't spend much time with him. Several years ago we worked together, and that is when I learned he had a high capacity for negativity and a low tolerance for hard work.

But I wanted to help Bill, so I was happy to look at his résumé. It's a good thing I was sitting down as I read it because you would have thought this guy was a high-performing, star employee. He had the right degree from a solid university, and his job experience was varied and convincing. The cover letter was professional and well written. If I didn't know Bill, I would have thought, *We better get this guy fast before someone else makes him a great offer!* But I know Bill—and I wouldn't hire him for any job, anywhere, at any time.

A résumé is almost completely worthless as a tool to rely on when hiring.

Think about it. Almost all résumés contain two categories of information: education and jobs held. Yet when I am hiring, those are the things I care the least about.

To make a hiring decision, I'd much rather know the following about the people I am interviewing:

- Skills. Have they developed aptitude for certain tasks?
- Leadership. Are there specific teams or projects (involving people) they successfully led?
- Capacity. Are they at their limit? Or is there room to learn and grow?
- Passion. Does the role being considered make their hearts beat fast?
- Heart. Do they love the church and wholeheartedly believe in its mission, vision, and values? Or in a business, do they believe in the vision and direction of the company?
- Character. Can I trust them?

In my two decades at Granger, I was involved in hiring more than one hundred staff members. We had very low turnover, and I think it is because of some core beliefs on how we hired. Here are four quick thoughts that helped our process when we interviewed new staff.

Chemistry Is Crucial

Chemistry is more important than skills, experience, or education. You have to play well in the sandbox with others. You must have some basic interpersonal skills. I've worked with some people in the past who were highly skilled, had great experience, and did their jobs well, but no one wanted to be around them. Chemistry was at the top of our criteria list. Of course, because we typically hired from within our organization (more on that later), we already knew if we liked the person we were hiring.

Formal Education Is Not a Priority

I think a great college education gets you your first job. It also can help you learn a good work ethic and develop some patterns for becoming a lifelong learner. Don't get me wrong; formal education is not a strike against you. It just was not very high on our list of criteria. We looked at chemistry, experience, and proven skills before we looked at education.

Pastor Dave Ferguson has also hired scores of church leaders, and he agrees: "The first qualification we look for in potential staff is 'proven faithfulness,' not formal theological education. We are definitely not against a formal theological education (I have one!), but that is not what we look for first when trying to find new staff."[1]

If you have a policy that requires a college education, do you realize you would have looked past great leaders like Abraham Lincoln, Christopher Columbus, Henry Ford, John D. Rockefeller, Walt Disney, Bill Gates, and Tim Stevens? I don't seriously consider myself a peer among these great leaders, but I do think you risk overlooking some tremendously effective leaders if you have requirements that pre-filter based on education.

Always Call References

Even if we had known the individual for twenty years, we called references. It's amazing to me that pastors don't do this. In my time at Granger, six staff members were hired away from us by other churches. Not one of those pastors ever called to ask questions about the individual's work ethic, attitude, strengths, weaknesses, or loyalty. And four of the six lasted at the new church less than three years before they were fired or left surrounded in a cloud of tension. With a simple call to us or other references, they would have known better how to set up their new staff members for success or possibly would have discovered they wouldn't be a great fit. Always call references.

Conduct Group Interviews

I'm pretty good with discernment and making good hiring decisions. However, I'm not as good by myself as I am with a group. That's why we always had a group of people involved in at least one interview with a potential hire. We selected people from across the organization who had shown they asked great questions, could help the candidate feel at ease, and had a gift of discernment.

There is no fail-safe way to guarantee a great hire. But following some important steps during the interview helps. As I wrote in *Simply Strategic Stuff*, you want long hellos and quick goodbyes.[2] Don't get those mixed up.

THINK ABOUT IT

1. If you have required a certain level of education for a position, revisit that decision. What is behind the requirement?

2. Are you experiencing a high turnover? If so, it might be due to some hiring practices that need to change. What might those be?

CHAPTER FIFTEEN

YOU CAN'T TRAIN CHARACTER

TEN YEARS AGO WE HIRED A TECHNICIAN TO LEAD OUR PRO-duction team and help with our services and events. He had all the right qualifications and was a joy to work with most of the time. But something that didn't show up on his résumé or in any of our reference calls was that he had a temper. About two months after he started, he got upset at a meeting and threw a table across the room as he stormed out. We gave him a warning, but it was only a couple of weeks before he got angry again and cussed out a volunteer loudly and publicly. This guy had a gaping character flaw, and we had to let him go.

Let me talk directly to church leaders first: This principle of choosing people of character can be a bit difficult for us. Why? *Because we are the church.* It is part of our business model to help pick up the pieces for people. It is our intention to be there when people fall so we can point them to Jesus and help get them back on their feet. If people in our church have addictions or bad habits, or if they engage in damaging behaviors, we don't kick them out of the church. We meet them where they are and help them take their next steps.

But when we are talking about volunteers or staff leaders, whom we have brought on the team to help others take steps, it is important that there aren't any debilitating character flaws that will cause others to stumble.

This can be misinterpreted by some to mean that only perfect people are allowed on the team. Nothing could be further from the truth. We don't want to encourage that kind of thinking or put that burden on our staff. All of us are dealing with something. All of us have areas in our lives where we need help and support. All of us deal with the reality of our humanity, and we are constantly striving to lean on Jesus.

But it's crucial that the people we bring on our team do not have huge flaws in their integrity that could cripple their ability to lead. Luke 12:48 says that more is required from those who have been given greater responsibility: "From everyone who has been given much, much will be demanded; and from the one who has been entrusted with much, much more will be asked." First Timothy 3 gives a whole list of requirements for leaders that is different—higher and more restrictive—from what is required of church attendees (vv. 1–13).

Even if you are leading a business, you want people of integrity on your team. You don't want to worry about whether money will go missing, customers will get mistreated, or a sexual harassment accusation will divert your focus.

Three Basic Areas

I'm not talking about unrealistic expectations; I'm talking about basic areas of integrity. In my experience, there are three big areas that seem to take leaders down over and over again.

WORDS

You don't want people on your team who can't control their tongues. James said, "By our speech we can ruin the world, turn harmony to chaos, throw mud on a reputation" (James 3:6 MSG). Whether you are trying to transform lives or deliver a product that will serve your customers, an employee who can't control his or her tongue will be detrimental to your bottom line.

MONEY

We live in a world that has little tolerance for financial mismanagement. It is important that you have policies to protect the assets of the organization, but it's also important that you have employees who are not mesmerized by money.

SEX

This is the big one, isn't it? It seems as if every week I hear of someone else who couldn't keep his or her pants zipped. This is not just a male issue. We've seen male and female leaders equally fall to sexual temptation. And it is damaging because it betrays trust and strips away credibility.

Caution and Precautions

So how do you make sure you don't hire someone with character flaws? You can't.

Even if you ask all the right questions and call all the references in advance, it doesn't mean someone won't fall. You are not responsible for someone else's personal choices, so don't beat yourself up if you have a member of your team who makes a bad choice.

If someone has fallen more than once to the same issue (such as an extramarital affair or embezzlement), it is much more likely that person will fall to it again. But there are some things you can do during the interview process to minimize the risk for yourself and your organization:

- Ask lots of questions up front of the candidates, their spouses, their references, and other close friends. You aren't looking for dirt, but if you find out about chinks in their armor, then you want to ask more questions.[1]
- Be very concerned when you hear about character flaws from others that the candidate didn't tell you about first. In my mind, that almost always disqualifies the person.
- Be less concerned when a candidate comes out and tells you right away, "This is what happened, and here is what I've done since then, and I encourage you to talk to anyone you want to ask more questions." That shows a strengthening character and authenticity, and that is attractive.
- When staff members do fall, do everything you can to restore them. They may not be able to stay on staff, but that does not relieve you of the responsibility to care for them (in the church world we call that "pastoring") through their recovery. Many times that means you are pressing through your own feelings of betrayal and abandonment, but it is something you must do. It gets even more difficult if they reject your help in favor of hiding and covering instead of coming clean.

In his book *Developing the Leader Within You*, John Maxwell quoted Thomas Macauley, the nineteenth-century British historian, who said, "The measure of a man's real character is what he would do if he would never be found out." Maxwell continued, "Life is like a vise; at times it will squeeze us. At those moments of pressure, whatever is inside will be found out. We cannot give what we do not have. Image promises much but produces little. Integrity never disappoints."[2]

Let's do everything we can to have men and women of integrity leading our organizations.

THINK ABOUT IT

1. Have you ever boldly asked a candidate, "If Satan was going to take you down, how would he do it?" How might this help?

2. Is there something in your own life that might trip you up down the road? Consider sharing this with someone.

CHAPTER SIXTEEN

SOCIAL MEDIA IS YOUR FRIEND

FACEBOOK. TWITTER. TUMBLR. INSTAGRAM. PINTEREST. BLOGS.
These social networking tools (and scores of others) have changed everything about hiring staff, finding volunteers, and leading people. Why? Because everything you've posted, tweeted, commented, e-mailed, sent, it's all out there. Seth Godin said it this way: "Google never forgets."[1]

A report from the University of Evansville seems to back this. They found that more and more employers are turning to the Internet to screen applicants. The study determined that employers were able to determine with a "surprising level of accuracy" personality traits and indicators that could predict future job performance.[2]

It worked for us. At Granger, before we hired people, we unapologetically researched them on Facebook, Twitter, and other sites. We discontinued our talks with potential staff members because of their online personas. We ignored applications because of what we'd found on the individuals' Facebook pages. We also fired people based on what we found online.

I would recommend doing some simple searches before you hire staff or select high-level volunteers. Here are some things to observe:

- Look through all their picture albums. You will learn much about people by the pictures they take and believe are worthy of posting.
- Read their posts to see how they think.
- Click on articles they link to and find out what they find interesting.
- See what they say about their spouses or kids.
- See if you can find how they react to people with whom they have a disagreement. Are they kind or critical? Do they treat people online the way you would want them to treat your leaders in person?
- See what they think is funny. Is it always crass and bordering on inappropriate? If so, that probably is a reflection of the heart.
- Find out about their interests. What movies do they like? What books do they read? Where do they like to vacation? What do they do when they have free time?

You might say, "That borders on stalking!" And you'd be exactly right. Stalking. Creeping. Whatever you want to call it . . . do it! Your work is way too important to chance getting someone on the team who has character flaws you don't know about. Anything that is put online is for public consumption. And it would be ridiculous not to do the fullest possible research. Be sure to focus on posts and content that come directly from your potential employee or volunteer. Posts made by other people risk being taken out of context or could contain false information.

If you were buying a used car, and they offered to give you the full historical report of every mechanical issue or accident the car had experienced, you would do it. You would want to know what you would be getting when you buy that car. If it is true when buying a car, it should be true when hiring team members and placing the entire credibility of the business or church behind their leadership.

Oh, and it probably goes without saying, but also make sure you are smart online. You might be ticked at the business where you last worked, but you'd do well not to air that online. Like Godin said, "Everything you do now ends up in your permanent record. The best plan is to overload Google with a long tail of good stuff and to always act as if you're on Candid Camera, because you are."[3]

THINK ABOUT IT

1. Do you need to change your hiring practice so you can begin intentionally cyber-stalking potential staff members?

2. Is there something you need to change about your personal online practices so they don't jeopardize a future opportunity?

CHAPTER SEVENTEEN

HIRING FROM WITHIN

THIS IS SUCH AN IMPORTANT PRINCIPLE THAT I'VE TALKED about it in numerous workshops and written about it in two previous books.[1] When you are ready to fill a position, always look within your business or church at the current volunteers and employees before you ever look outside.

This is contrary to how most places hire. Most believe that they need someone from outside to take them to "the next level." Or churches figure they need the expertise and skills of someone coming from seminary. Or they need someone to challenge the status quo and help them figure out new and different ways to do business. Or they need someone who has been where they want to go.

All this may be true, and a new person may indeed turn out to be best, but there are several things that you must also factor into the decision before you look outside. These are areas that most businesses and churches forget to consider:

You Can't Underestimate Your Organization's DNA

There are things that make your organization unique. Yes, this includes your written mission, vision, and values statements, but it also includes personalities, leadership styles, and cultures. It includes many things that will never be captured on paper. It's the stuff you can't always ask your out-of-town candidate to agree to. They are often the intangibles, and the incompatibility of an outsider may not appear for months or years.

You Can't Underestimate Chemistry

This may be one of the most overlooked areas in hiring. You have to like your team. You have to enjoy the people you are working with. If someone is coming to oversee your music ministry, you must be reasonably certain that the volunteers in that area will like the new person and want to work with him. If you hire someone from within, you already know about her relationships with the people around her. You can already see the respect that she's earned and the influence she's gained.

You Can't Overestimate Authenticity

You can ask all the questions you want in the interview, you can do a dozen different tests, and you can call a hundred references, but you still don't get close to the truth about people until you live with them and watch them in everyday life. You need to see her when she is squeezed and when she's attacked. You need to watch him when everything falls apart at the last minute or when his budget gets slashed to almost nothing. When you hire a faithful and proven volunteer, or transfer an employee from another department, you have significantly reduced your chances of being surprised.

———

At Granger, 119 of our 127 staff members were hired from among our volunteers. Of the ten pastors, eight were hired from within the church. In Granger's twenty-eight-year history, 95 percent of the inside hires were successful. That means they are still on staff or they left without difficulty. Only *50 percent* of the outside hires were successful.

Hiring from within is a principle that we embraced whole-heartedly during my time at Granger and is one of the reasons we had such low staff turnover. When you have low turnover, you can focus more time on the core of your business and less on staff replacement issues.

Don Reynolds was a network administrator before becoming one of our staff worship leaders. Melanie Rosander ran a restaurant and is now overseeing all the operations of the church. Tony Morgan was a city manager before I hired him to be a pastor at Granger. Jason Miller was a senior in college when we asked him to step into a huge role as one of our pastors. And all of them were volunteering their time in one of our ministries. I was also a volunteer at Granger before I joined the staff.

Advantages of Hiring Within

Dave Ferguson is the lead pastor at Community Christian Church in Naperville, Illinois, where they also practice hiring from within. He said there are seven advantages of hiring a person from among your base of volunteers or current employees:

1. You can observe his character before hiring.
2. You can observe his proven faithfulness before hiring.
3. You can observe her giftedness in action before hiring.
4. She understands and buys into your philosophy of ministry!
5. He understands and buys into your vision!
6. He loves your church!
7. She will offer a lot fewer surprises![2]

So think about it. You may already have people in your organization who have proven integrity and character. They understand your vision and have a high capacity for growth. They have proven themselves to be leaders, and they may even have grown to love you and demonstrate faithfulness in their current roles. They're enjoyable to be around, and they have skills you need. My recommendation: hire them as soon as you can!

THINK ABOUT IT

1. Church leaders: Who do you know is an amazing volunteer, but you've hesitated hiring that person because he or she lacks professional church experience?

2. Business leaders: Do you have a system of identifying entry-level employees who have a far greater capacity than the role they are currently filling?

3. Do you have high staff turnover? If so, why?

CHAPTER EIGHTEEN
FRESH EYES

IF YOU ARE READING THIS BOOK IN ORDER, YOU ARE GOING to get to the end of this chapter and think I'm schizophrenic. Because now I'm going to tell you the exact opposite of what I said in the previous chapter on hiring from within your organization.

The reality is, sometimes you should *not* hire from within; you may need a fresh perspective and new ideas. Frankly, you might need someone who doesn't think like your team.

Paul Alexander said it this way: "When you need to shift the culture, philosophy, strategy or you don't have the new skills needed for the role within, then hire from outside. The outside hire will bring an infusion of new ideas and fresh eyes that you'll benefit greatly from."[1]

Scott Williams called it the "Inbred Syndrome."[2] He says it is one of the major reasons that big companies fail; they are unwilling to bring outside people into the organization to infuse new ideas.

A couple of years before I left Granger, we engaged the services of an outside search firm for the first time in our history to help us with a key hire.[3] I entered that arrangement with trepidation. I was already anxious that we were considering hiring for this position from outside when so many of our greatest staff members had come from inside. But the fear really set in when I began considering handing off the search process to people (i.e., "experts") whom I didn't know very well.

But we did this because we needed their help. We were moving toward a brand-new vision for the church that required us to think differently. We knew that if we kept doing what had worked in the past, we'd keep getting the same results, heading in the same direction. We believed finding a few key people from outside could be exactly what we needed to give us the momentum required to accomplish the gargantuan vision that God had given us.

When you are hiring from the outside, there are some things you should know about your new hire:

- She will initially require much more of your time than an inside hire.
- There will be times you might wonder, *Does he really get it?* as he is grappling with your culture.
- She will question systems, ideas, and values that no one else questions. Some of her questions will require answers or training. Other questions will require you to consider changing something that isn't working or doesn't make sense.
- You will need a process to infuse your values and company DNA into him over a period of months, not days. This isn't a go-to-a-workshop-and-you-are-done deal. This will take intentionality over a long period of time.
- It takes two to three years for an outside hire to be settled and comfortable.
- You will have to work extra hard so his spouse doesn't feel isolated. If you want him to stay long term, it is crucial to help his entire family acclimate to their new location. You may see your new staff member come to work every day

and make all kinds of new friends, not realizing his wife is at home with the kids, making very few friends, feeling miserable because of everything she gave up.

Whether you decide to hire from within, or to get some fresh eyes, it's not a one-time decision. You must reevaluate it with every hire, deciding what is most important for your next steps as an organization.

THINK ABOUT IT

1. Is your business or church stuck? Do you need some staff with fresh eyes in key positions to help you get out of a rut? If so, in what ways, specifically?

2. Have you decided what's not negotiable about your company culture or practices? When a new hire pushes back or asks questions, what is open for discussion and what is not?

CHAPTER NINETEEN

QUESTIONS TO ASK

SEVERAL YEARS AGO I WITNESSED A BAD VEHICLE ACCI-
dent when a passenger van crashed into the side of a semitruck that
was blocking the road. Months later I was involved in a deposition
where I had to give sworn testimony to what I saw. I walked away
from that experience marveling at the quantity and detail of the
questions thrown at me by the attorney: "What time was it? Were
there any houses nearby? What color were the houses? Did you see
any light poles? How many? Were the lights on or off? So you are
saying all of them were off? Were any cars parked on the street?
How many and what color and what models?"

And on it went for a couple of hours. A good attorney or a good
reporter will ask questions others wouldn't think to ask. And so
they uncover information others don't uncover.

An interview isn't a deposition, but there is still a responsibility to ask solid questions so you can learn everything you need to
know to make a good decision. I've learned a great deal watching the skillful handling of group interviews conducted by my
coworkers. Following is a list of great questions you should consider asking your next job candidate:

1. *When were you excited about your work?* This reveals what motivates your candidate. You want a person whose passions align with the job description.
2. *What major mistakes from your past do you* not *regret?* From great failures come big lessons, so look for employees who recognize the importance of messing up.
3. *What's your favorite movie?* Remember, chemistry matters. It's good to know what candidates enjoy doing. If not movies, perhaps they can tell you about books they have read or music they enjoy.
4. *What's a misconception people have about you?* You want employees who understand how they come across to other people.
5. *How happy are you in your current job?* Look for people who are very happy at their jobs, or if not, who don't talk negatively about their work environments or current employers. It's all about attitude, which, you may have heard, is a choice.
6. *If you weren't interviewing for this role, is there another role here you'd be interested in?* I want to know if candidates are just trying to get their foot in the door, or if they really are passionate about this role.
7. *If I were to ask your current boss what your greatest strengths are, what would he or she say?* This is another way to ask about strengths without candidates feeling as if they are bragging.
8. *If I were to ask your current boss what you do that drives him or her crazy, what would your boss say?* This is another way to get at weaknesses or idiosyncrasies.
9. *Do you have any fears about this position or work environment?* If the candidate has none, he or she might be too cocky or unclear on what you are asking.
10. *Why do you want to work here?* You want people who have a real passion to be on your team. It can't be just a job; it's got to make their heart beat fast.

11. *Describe the boss who would get the very best from you.* This allows you to hear a little bit about the work environment they enjoy.
12. *Tell me about a time you had to be especially bold or honest in a work situation, despite the potential risk.* Maybe the candidate will be in your face all the time, or perhaps he or she will never speak up. You will want to know either way.
13. *Let's assume you take this job, and one year from now you go home after work feeling like this was the best decision of your life. What happened during that year to make you think that?* This helps you get to some of the candidate's unstated expectations or dreams.
14. *Describe a time you were asked to do something you didn't know how to do.* Is this a person who needs step-by-step instructions for every task or someone who is self-motivated to find the answer?
15. *Tell me about a time a boss asked you to do something you didn't agree with, and how you responded.* This will help you gauge the candidate's interpersonal skills and ability to navigate conflict.
16. *Tell me more.* I learned this from my good friend Mark Waltz as a phrase you can say after just about every question. It helps pull things out of a candidate who isn't very chatty.
17. *Do you have any questions for us?* Beware of individuals who come to a meeting and have no questions, especially if they are just getting to know you or the organization.

And a few more questions to ask if you are hiring for a church or faith-based organization:

18. *Tell us your faith story. When did you meet Jesus?* You want to know the candidate can articulate his or her story. If the

person has been a follower for many years, you also want to hear signs of recent spiritual steps.

19. *Is there anything we should know about you or your past that would have the potential of hurting the cause of Christ or the church if revealed later?* This is a question that should be asked one-on-one, not in a group, and by someone of the same gender. It's a hard question to ask, but you really do need to know the answer.

20. If his or her spouse is in an interview: *What's the greatest fear you have about your husband (or wife) taking this job?* I want to make sure they are in this together, and that I know about any concerns the spouse might have.[1]

THINK ABOUT IT

1. Which question made you think, *Oh, that's good!* Why?

2. Do you currently have an environment where you could ask these types of questions when interviewing a candidate? If not, what could you change?

CHAPTER TWENTY

JOB DESCRIPTIONS

I'M NOT A BIG FAN OF JOB DESCRIPTIONS IN THE WORK-place. When used for employees already on the payroll, they are intended to replace face-to-face interaction and give us something to point to when someone isn't doing his or her job. I'd rather not create a culture where we pull out a piece of paper to put in someone's face instead of addressing a problem.

Evidently I'm not alone. Alexander Kjerulf, the self-described "Happiness Officer," gave five reasons why he believes job descriptions are useless:

1. Nobody reads them anyway. Do you? I thought not. I never did. Very few people do. Some companies don't even have them, and they seem to manage just fine.
2. They're always incomplete. Nobody's job description contains all the crucial things they do or all their important responsibilities. There's always more to it than is captured on paper. If everybody in the company did only what it says in their job description, the company would soon grind to a halt.
3. They're a hassle to create and maintain. They're actually a

lot of work to write and especially to update.

4. They're usually obsolete. Most people's jobs change a lot faster than their job descriptions. In many cases the job description only says what the job used to be like a long time ago—you know, way back in the last quarter.

5. They don't help people do their jobs. I don't think a single person has ever told me, "Today I accomplished something at work that I couldn't possibly have done without my job description." They're close to useless in day-to-day operations.[1]

When Descriptions Actually Are Needed

I do think, however, that job descriptions are helpful when you are hiring someone new or transitioning someone to a new role. They help set expectations and establish benchmarks to define the beginning of your work relationship.

There are five categories that I think are important to include on any job description:

1. The type of person for this specific role
2. Personal values or character qualities that are important
3. A description of the job's duties
4. How success is defined
5. Reporting structure

To make this practical, I thought I'd share an actual job description that we created for the position of campus pastor (in the business world, this is kind of like a branch manager) at Granger. You will find four of the five categories above included (I left off reporting structure for the purposes of this illustration):

ROLE: THE CAMPUS PASTOR IS A . . .

- Catalytic leader: able to rally people to a cause.
- Team builder: can build teams and identify high-capacity leaders to build more teams.
- Relational leader: friendly and approachable.
- Talent scout: always on the lookout for new leaders and volunteers.
- Total quality manager: looking for ways to improve; sensitive to misses; committed to excellence.
- Communicator: the primary host, greeter, and vision-caster of this congregation.
- Cheerleader: encouraging volunteers and staff constantly.
- Carrier of the DNA: when you cut this person, he or she bleeds the mission, vision, and values of the organization.
- Solution specialist: able to identify problems and find solutions.
- Staff champion: cares for the spiritual, emotional, and familial health of campus staff.
- Pastor: has a heart to identify leaders and build systems to care for the congregation.
- Reproducer: with the entire staff, reproduces leaders, followers of Christ, and campuses.

PERSONALLY: THE CAMPUS PASTOR IS A . . .

- Learner: can take direction and feedback well and has a great desire to learn.
- Seasoned: knows and loves our organization; no question on understanding method or philosophy.
- Conflict resolver: unafraid to tackle interpersonal conflicts, ministry misalignment, or issues of sin.

- Leader at home: no concerning spiritual or emotional health issues within his or her family.
- Time manager: does not require external systems to prioritize; is intrinsically motivated.
- Person of integrity: at the core, he or she makes solid decisions based on lifelong values.
- Self-aware individual: knows where he or she is weak; finds others to fill in those gaps.
- Disciple: fully devoted to following Jesus in everything he or she does.

JOB: THE CAMPUS PASTOR . . .

- Pastors: helps meet the care needs of his or her growing congregation. Some of this is done personally. As the church grows, much of this is done by developing systems of care and equipping leaders to help.
- Is present: keeps a presence in the community where the campus is located. Lives near enough to easily be available to hold meetings or respond to needs in the community.
- Builds teams: identifies, equips, empowers, and leads volunteers to do the ministry of the church at this campus.
- Connects: attends the all-staff meeting at the main campus each week; meets with members of the lead team as requested.
- Communicates: keeps his or her supervisor aware of the successes and struggles taking place at the site by proactively and consistently sharing stories and reports.
- Is an expert: learns the people, issues, needs, concerns, history, and demographics of the community.
- Is flexible: jumps in to help wherever needed at any of the church campuses or ministries.

- Is a team player: adheres to the staff handbook, which includes a statement of ethics.
- Follows: a leader, yes, but also a follower who will do everything possible to make his or her supervisor, the senior pastor, and the church leadership a success.

SUCCESS OF A CAMPUS IS DEFINED BY . . .

- Making disciples: people are meeting Jesus and growing in their faith.
- Passionate alignment: there is excitement about the vision of our church.
- Growing intentionally: every year more people are attending, meeting Christ, taking steps, and participating than were in the previous year.
- Financial health: within twelve months, the revenue coming in matches or exceeds the expenses going out. Within twenty-four months, the excess revenue coming in has paid for the start-up expenses.
- Volunteer development: the ministry is led by capable, trained, and aligned volunteers.
- Collaborative creativity: the campus becomes a petri dish for creativity and innovation, and the ministry that flourishes is shared with all the other campuses.

This job description likely looks very different from what you would need for a position you are hiring for, especially in business. However, the categories are important. It not only gives your candidate an idea of your expectations, but it also forces you to think about the type of person you want and the job he or she will be performing.

THINK ABOUT IT

1. Think through Alexander Kjerulf's list of why job descriptions are useless internally. Do you agree or disagree? Why?

2. Do your job descriptions include value and integrity statements like the illustration above? How might this benefit you?

CHAPTER TWENTY-ONE

FIND LEADERS, NOT DOERS

I'M GOING TO TELL YOU A CLASSIC STORY I'VE HEARD several times. I can't give credit because I have no idea where it originated, but it goes something like this:

> The owner of a car dealership was looking at his sales reports one day and noticed that Tom Phelps was outselling every other salesperson. Tom had been on the team just a short time, and yet he was closing sales left and right. In fact, in the previous month he doubled the sales of both Bob Jenkins and Laura Budowski, who had been known for years as the top-producing employees in the company.
>
> Month after month, the owner watched this trend continue. He visited the sales floor and watched Tom work his magic. He was aggressive, but customers didn't feel violated. He was friendly, but not in a way that was over-the-top. And perhaps most important, he had gained the respect of his coworkers, which is nearly impossible in a competitive selling environment.
>
> The owner was seeing profits steadily increase. He wanted to find a way to take a little of who Tom was and infuse it in

the rest of the company at all his dealerships. He also wanted to honor Tom for the value he was bringing to the company.

So after six months with a proven track record of outperforming every other employee in the history of the company, Tom Phelps was given a promotion. He was elevated to sales manager of his location, and also would oversee the sales managers at every other location. The owner couldn't wait to see Tom's enthusiasm and sales techniques catch fire across the entire company.

When the next month's sales reports came out, the owner was a bit surprised. Sales were pretty flat. No increase at all. He excused it since Tom hadn't really had a chance to get settled yet. Next month would be better.

And yet the following month the sales had actually decreased. By the fourth month sales were back to the level they were prior to when Tom arrived at the company. Eventually Tom resigned in frustration, having lost the respect of the owner and his associates.

———————

What happened? The owner of this dealership made a classic mistake based on a faulty assumption. He assumed that because Tom was a good doer, Tom would also be a good leader. He took an amazing sales guy off the floor where he loved meeting people and stuck him in an office with no windows, and expected him to know how to reproduce himself in others.

Sounds ridiculous, right? And yet how many times do we make the same mistake when hiring staff? We have a guy who plays guitar and has a great voice, and when the church gets big enough that we can finally hire a worship leader, we ask this guy to join the team. That's okay if we have the luxury of a budget that can afford paying a guy to play guitar and sing (or to be a doer), but if what we really need is someone who can build teams so we have twenty musicians at the end of the first year, then we may need to look for someone else.

At the church where I worked, when we needed to hire someone to oversee our IT department, it would have been natural to find someone who could administrate networks, fix computers, and write code. But it would not have worked to have that kind of person overseeing the more than 250 computers and devices that we supported. Instead, we found Jason Powell, a high school physics teacher who had a good understanding in all the areas of IT, but more than that, he had a proven track record of overseeing lots of people and building teams. Today, he's not the guy who knows more than anyone else about computers. But because he is wired as a *leader* rather than a *doer*, he has built a team (with one staff member—the rest are volunteers).

This chapter may sound as if I place a higher value on leaders than doers. Nothing could be further from the truth. Let me clarify.

I'm not saying leaders are more valuable than doers. It is not about value; it is about role. When you have limited dollars, you need every penny to count. If you hire a staff member to do something, you get forty-five to fifty hours of productive ministry done every week. But if you hire people who can multiply themselves through recruiting volunteers and building teams, you might get two hundred, four hundred, or a thousand hours of productive work done every week.

I'm not saying there is no place for doers in a church or organization. We needed hundreds, even thousands, of doers in our church. We needed people to lead small groups, take care of the building, answer the phones, plan games for students, set up chairs, maintain equipment, tune sound systems, and so much more.

I'm not saying every position in your organization should be filled by a leader. Again, not true. Churches and businesses need far more doers than leaders. If every position were open only to a person who has been wired by God as a leader, then many of those people would leave unfulfilled. We need many people who are comfortable in the fact that God has wired them as doers, and who find their fulfillment in serving, loving, and helping.

I am saying that God has called the church to be effective. Churches have limited time and money, so it is especially important that every staff member hired brings the highest return for the kingdom of God in that community. This is the reason Ephesians 4 says the purpose of a pastor is "to equip his people for works of service, so that the body of Christ may be built up" (v. 12). It is the job of pastors to equip. If the job of church leaders were to *do* the ministry, that verse would not be in the Bible.

Most staff positions should be filled by staff members who are leaders. It is only when a church begins to get large that it should consider hiring doers for such roles as helping maintain the facility or offering administrative assistance to a pastor.

THINK ABOUT IT

1. Have you ever been frustrated because a doer was in a position that should have been filled by a leader? Describe the situation.

2. Do you feel as if your church or nonprofit organization communicates that leaders are more important than doers? If so, how could this be changed?

CHAPTER TWENTY-TWO

THE DYNAMIC TENSION BETWEEN CREATIVES AND LEADERS

"HE JUST DOESN'T GET IT!" PASTOR CALVIN GENTRY exclaimed as I left his office.

I'd just wrapped up an hour-long conversation with Calvin about his worship leader, Jeff. I hadn't intended on doing a counseling session during my visit to Northside Church—I was just passing through town. But following the Sunday service, as I was talking with both Calvin and Jeff in the offices, the tension was so thick you could cut it with a knife. I knew I needed to stay for a couple of days.

I had long-standing relationships with both Calvin and Jeff for many years; Calvin and I went to school together, and Jeff was an intern with me about ten years earlier. So I'd kept up with both of them, and when Calvin was looking for a worship leader two years ago, I did not hesitate to recommend Jeff.

Now I wasn't sure. I'd spent the prior evening with Jeff and heard him unload a truckload of complaints and frustrations about working under Pastor Gentry. I'll have to admit that some of the stuff he said made me think the problem might be with Calvin.

But after I spent some time with Calvin, I could see things

from a different perspective. In fact, the whole conflict existed because each one was only seeing through his own eyes. They were speaking, reacting, interpreting, and then overreacting because of their wiring. Calvin had no idea how to work with creatives, and Jeff was at a loss as to how to work under a charge-up-the-hill type of leader.

———

After more than two decades in ministry, I've seen this scenario repeated over and over. The names change. The locations are different. But the bottom line remains: there is a dynamic tension between those wired as creatives (designers, musicians, artists) and those wired as leaders (CEOs, administrators, senior pastors). Sometimes this is explained as right-brain wiring (intuitive, creative, expresses emotions easily) versus left-brain wiring (logical, analytical, good at reasoning).

In business it is often the engineers who are frustrated by the design department. Or the developers who can't see eye to eye with those in marketing. It's just a fact: the tension exists. You can wish it wasn't there. You can hope it will go away. But the tension is real. And the tension must be managed. If it isn't, it will drive a wedge in your organization and will cause many teams to divide. Or worse yet, you will just put up with one another and begin merely to exist.

The problem? Creatives and leaders are different.

- Creatives want to help people have an experience. Leaders want to give them facts or information.
- Creatives want the freedom to try stuff, the chance to risk. Leaders personally like risk, but when it comes to planning a service or launching a product, they want to know what is happening and be fairly confident it's going to work.

- Creatives are feelers. Leaders are thinkers.
- Creatives have a hard time logically explaining how the artistic elements will contribute to the goal; they just feel strongly that it will work. Leaders have difficulty investing time or money based on a feeling.
- Creatives like asking questions. Leaders like giving answers.
- Creatives like leaving the audience in the tension of the unanswered. Leaders feel as if they are failing if they don't offer a convincing message.
- Creatives want to be a part of the dreaming phase. They want to know the "why" and not just the "what." Leaders want to hire someone to create a product around their concepts.

Before you say it, I realize these statements are filled with generalities. There are many creatives who are great leaders. And there are plenty of leaders who have the heart of an artist. But the differences are clear.

God has uniquely gifted creatives to take us to places we would otherwise never go. In church, they can usher us into the presence of God in a few short minutes when it would take us hours to get there on our own. In business, they can help us feel something in a commercial that we weren't even thinking about thirty seconds earlier. Creatives help us feel more deeply and experience more fully. They take a truth that has found its way into our heads and create an opportunity for it to be driven deep into our hearts. An artist will write a song, poem, or script; another will deliver the words with an unfiltered rawness of gift and emotion; and still others will masterfully mix the image or sound so I see and hear it clearly.

Left-brain leaders are gifted no less. Many of them are teachers; they listen, learn, and speak the truth to us even when it isn't popular. Leaders are passionate about driving the mission deep into the hearts of the people. In the church, they keep their ears open to hear from God, then communicate the vision in such a way to rally artists and others to a greater purpose. Leaders are never satisfied with the way things are; they can only see how things should be, the way things could be.

The creative and the leader can be focused on the same mission, yet so differently; they can be serving the same cause, yet often hold opposing views on how to call others to do the same. This may be the single most important relationship to navigate in any church or business. And unfortunately, most leaders never figure out how to make it work.

The result? Anger, bitterness, ugly departures, sometimes even church splits or business failures.

I don't want to pretend this is an easy issue to solve, but I can offer some suggestions to keep this relationship working:

- Leaders: Let your creatives take risks. The only way to do this is to give them room to create.
- Leaders: Stop micromanaging. This sucks the life out of your creatives.
- Creatives: Learn how to lead up. Remove emotion from your argument and try to speak the language of your leader.
- Both: Spend time together. This is the only way to really begin to trust each other and learn what is important to the other.
- Creatives: Communicate well and often. Don't assume others will feel it.
- Leaders: Let your creatives participate in the planning. They need to know the reasons behind the plans, not just the bottom line.
- Creatives: Respect your leader.

- Leaders: Affirm your creatives today, tomorrow, and the next day.
- Creatives: You need to affirm your leader. He or she comes across as more confident than he or she truly is.

So embrace the tension. Just because the relationship is hard does not mean it isn't worth it. I've seen too many creatives quit in frustration because they give up too soon. I've seen too many leaders fire or drive away a valuable member of their team because they refuse to stop for a moment and see through another person's eyes.

Creatives and leaders, it doesn't have to be a perfect storm. I could say that you can make a beautiful rainbow together, but that would be cheesy. So I'll close by saying *work it out.*[1]

THINK ABOUT IT

1. Leaders: Have you had a high turnover of artistic staff? If so, what is it about your style or practices as a leader that is making it difficult for artists to stick around?

2. Creatives: What can you improve so that you are leading up more effectively?

CHAPTER TWENTY-THREE

PAY WELL

YOU HARDLY EVER HEAR CHURCH LEADERS TALK ABOUT compensation. It's almost like the topic is off limits. And yet it is clear from 1 Corinthians 9:13–14 that those who work in the ministry should make their living from those who are receiving the ministry. "You know, don't you, that it's always been taken for granted that those who work in the Temple live off the proceeds of the Temple, and that those who offer sacrifices at the altar eat their meals from what has been sacrificed? Along the same lines, the Master directed that those who spread the Message be supported by those who believe the Message" (MSG). I believe it honors God when we take care of those who take care of us. And this doesn't just apply to the church. I have friends in business who see it as a blessing to be able to provide great jobs for good people. Their passion goes beyond offering a product and making money—they want to contribute to the community through providing well-paying positions.

Here is what I think:

You don't want staff to *join* because of money.

It would be sad to have someone on staff because you offered the person so much money that he or she couldn't possibly turn it down. You want people to join the team because the mission and vision compel them to come. You want them to join because they can't imagine working anywhere else. You want from them an attitude of "I'd work there for free if I could!" while your attitude is "I want to pay them as much as I possibly can!"

You don't want staff to *stay* because of money.

I've talked with church staff members who weren't excited about their jobs anymore. They had eyes for other places they would love to work and said to me, "Honestly, I'm staying because I can't match what I'm making anywhere else. The health insurance isn't as good, and I wouldn't have as many vacation days." What a poor reason to stay on a staff. You want to pay people really well, but you don't want to pay them so much they would stay on the team even after they lost the passion for the vision.

You don't want staff to *leave* because of money.

Let's be honest: life is hard. And as a leader, you don't want it to be any more difficult for your staff families. It should be important that your core staff is well compensated. You don't want them to have to think about leaving because they can't cover their basic needs like groceries, clothing, house payments, or gas bills. That isn't to say they won't struggle financially—this happens for all kinds of reasons, such as poor money decisions, unmanageable debt, and lifestyle choices (e.g., sending children to private school or having a parent be able to stay home with the kids)—but you want to make sure your core staff does not have to leave due to the inability to take care of their basic needs.

PAY WELL

The Bible doesn't tell CEOs how much they should pay their employees, nor does it tell lead pastors how much they should pay their pastors or directors. In the church, you don't want to pay salaries that are much higher or much lower from what an average person brings home in your community. Instead, you want to provide salaries that are at the high end of the average wage. That is, they are a little bit higher than the average person in the community makes. I believe Scripture supports this when it says of church leaders, "Give a bonus to leaders who do a good job, especially the ones who work hard at preaching and teaching" (1 Tim. 5:17 MSG).

This means that sometimes very difficult decisions have to be made. At Granger in early 2009, in the depths of the recession, we had to eliminate eight positions from our staff. We were asked, "Why didn't you just cut all salaries by 20 percent rather than eliminating eight positions?" The reason was driven by the value we placed on paying well. We wanted to take good care of every person whom we could afford to have on staff. For the eight who left, we determined to take good care of them as they transitioned to other employment. For those who stayed, they didn't get raises that year, but we continued to provide well for their families.

We also sometimes had to reduce department budgets so we could increase salaries. There were many occasions when we decided there was more value in rewarding the staff who have been faithful, while at the same time giving those same staff members less money in their departmental budgets.

Three things to note while you are determining compensation:

1. It's important that you don't have people making decisions about salaries who have a "vow of poverty" mind-set. This sometimes happens in the church world. It's okay if someone believes that everyone in ministry should live like a pauper,

but you don't want that person on your board deciding how much the youth pastor should make.

2. No one should ever determine his or her own compensation. The employee in question should not even be in the room when it is discussed.

3. We hardly had any rules at Granger, but a critical one was "do not talk about your compensation with anyone else in the organization." Comparison and jealousy can tear a team apart quicker than just about anything else. And it is insidious. In the Bible there is a story about workers in a vineyard. They were perfectly happy to work all day for one dollar; that is, until they heard the workers who started late in the day were getting paid the same. It was the comparison that made them angry enough to complain to their boss (Matt. 20:1–16).

There are some good church salary and business salary surveys available to help you set compensation, and you should check your local city or county to find out what is average in your community.[1]

THINK ABOUT IT

1. How do you think your business or church is doing right now with its compensation plan?

2. Are you currently caught up in the comparison trap because you know how much someone else makes? Consider confessing this and asking God for the grace to be content with what he has given you.

CHAPTER TWENTY-FOUR

IT'S MESSY WHEN YOU WORK WITH YOUR FRIENDS

SEVERAL YEARS AGO I WAS HELPING A LEADER THROUGH some strategic decisions. His organization had stopped growing, and it was beginning to lose good staff members. He was trying to figure out what needed to change to reverse the trend.

He was telling me stories that illustrated the problem and said some of the staff members who left felt he was distant and unavailable. He said to me in frustration, "I don't want to be their friend. I just want them to do their &%@$ job!"

This is a guy who had been burned by working with friends. And if you've been in leadership for very long, you've also been burned.

About ten years ago, I was beginning a tough conversation with a friend who had worked with me for a long time. He had been an amazing leader, helping grow one of our departments to a significant level. But the pace of growth and change was beginning to stretch his capacity, and I felt there might need to be a new leader in place. I had not made it far in the conversation when he blurted out, "You are going to fire me, aren't you?" Once that was in his mind, there was no convincing him otherwise. He angrily left my office that day, and I haven't seen him since. I didn't just lose an employee; I lost a friend. I had an especially tight connection with his entire family, and I lost them all as friends that day.

Another time I had to let a close friend go for financial reasons. We could no longer afford to keep her on staff. I had become sort of a father figure to her, and it was incredibly painful to see her go. I had hoped she and I could keep up the friendship, and I could continue to help her grow and succeed. But I soon realized she no longer wanted me in her life.

Those types of experiences are what cause people to say, "Never again. I will never hire another friend, and I will keep a distance so I don't get too close to the people I work with." We think, *It's just not worth the pain.*

I get that. I don't like pain. I don't like losing friends. Just as a little kid who gets burned by touching the stove stays away from it, I want to get as far away as possible from it. Why even go in the kitchen again? If I don't go in the kitchen, the stove can't burn me.

And yet I've learned over the years that the benefits of working with friends far outweigh the potential pain. Being able to do ministry with people I love being around is a rare joy that few people get to experience. Going to work with people I like, and who like me, and who are fun to hang with—I wouldn't trade those benefits.

Even amid the painful stories, I have had far more long-lasting friendships with people who, although we no longer work together, continue to be close friends to this day. When you are working with friends, it takes a much higher commitment to communication. Sometimes you have to say out loud, "Right now I'm wearing my leader hat. In a few minutes I'll put my friend hat back on." Sometimes I've said, "As your friend I would advise you in one way, but as your employer I would counsel you differently."

Recently I said to a friend (who also worked for me), "Someone repeated something you said about my leadership last week, and it's been eating at me. It really hurt, but I realized it was unfair to assume they were representing you accurately. Can we talk about it?"

Without that level of commitment to honesty, stuff builds up and friendships erode. Working in a place where friendships once existed but are now tense is worse than starting at a place where everyone is just an associate.

I know it's messy when you choose to work with your friends. In the church, I don't know how we model true disciple-making communities without doing so at the staff level. And for Christian leaders in the business world, you have the opportunity to show others how followers of Jesus love through work relationships—caring for one another and pushing through the conflict that occasionally arises. Yeah, it's messy.

As for me, I choose the mess.

THINK ABOUT IT

1. Have you ever had a working relationship with a friend end poorly? Has this caused you to build up any walls toward people you work with now?

2. Is there someone you need to have an honest conversation with even if you know it might hurt him or her, or yourself? What can you do about it?

CHAPTER TWENTY-FIVE

LEAVE WELL

ONE OF THE IMPORTANT BUT NOT VERY FUN PARTS OF MY job at Granger was having tough conversations with employees (i.e., "friends"), which sometimes ended with terminating their jobs. I always had a pit in my stomach while working through these difficult transitions.

I liked having a team that was unified, focused, and competent in their roles. I hated having to dismiss a staff member who was no longer contributing toward a healthy culture.

I loved celebrating a staff member who soared in his role and helped his team win. I hated when, a couple of years later, that same staffer had lost his energy, developed a bad attitude, and reached a lid on his capacity to lead.

I was not surprised those conversations were filled with emotion. I was not surprised when the person receiving the news cried, got upset, and said something in the moment he or she didn't really mean.

However, what shocked me again and again was when, days or weeks later, I heard bitter words of entitlement come from the individual.

"I worked there for five years—I can't believe they fired me."

"I was screwed!"

"I'm too old to find another job, yet the church just abandoned me."

"I'll never step foot in that place again after they stabbed me in the back like that."

I know of former staffers still emotionally crippled a year after their employments ended, overwhelmed with anger and bitterness over no longer being employed by the church.

It's interesting to me because most of them attended the church for years before joining the staff team. They volunteered, served, and worshiped for a long time without being compensated. Most of them experienced a significant spiritual moment (or many moments) through the ministry of the church.

But somehow when money entered the equation, and then was removed, the sense of entitlement crept up and entangled people and clouded their perspectives. It was almost as if the church owed them jobs; as if the mission of the organization was not to be effective or good stewards of limited money, but rather to keep people employed.

I have a fair number of issues or disagreements with Fox News, and with Dick Morris, but I thought his response after being fired by Fox was stellar.

In February 2013, Dick was interviewed on the *Piers Morgan Show* on CNN. Of course, being the chief competitor to Fox News, Piers was anxious to hear Dick diminish his former employer. He pushed and prodded, hoping to get a response.

He asked, "Why you? . . . Did they want to make you a poster child? . . . A lot of people at Fox News were wrong. Why single you out?"

Dick took the blame twice by saying, "I was wrong at the top of my lungs, and that's why."

That wasn't good enough for Piers; he wanted some trash: "Do you resent that they pushed you out?"

He was trying to get past the facts and talk about the emotion. I loved Dick's response: "Look, Fox News gave me the opportunity of a lifetime . . . fifteen years, three thousand interviews. At some point the great marriage has to come to an end."

Still not satisfied, Piers then took another full minute to speak poorly about the Fox News Channel, citing falling market share and baiting Dick to say something bad about his employer. But he didn't take the bait.

He diverted the question by replying, "Regardless of whether you want to blame Fox News or not, I believe the problems are . . ." and then began to outline issues with political parties, changing culture, and more.[1]

I hope you never get fired—I hope I don't either. But if it happens, it would be smart to respond the same way Dick did.

A Graceful Exit

Here is a list of principles to consider when leaving a position:

- It is not disingenuous or fake to keep your mouth shut. You don't have to say everything you are thinking to every person who asks.
- Focus on the good years, not the bad days. Just as Morgan did with Dick Morris, people who want you to say something spiteful will bait you. Instead, focus on everything good that came out of your tenure.
- If you need to talk, and you probably will, save it for your spouse, a far-removed friend, or a counselor. If you worked for a church, don't talk to anyone in the church or any former work associate about your issues.
- Your future employer will pay attention to how you talk about your former employer. The things stated

on Facebook, Twitter, and all other social media are permanent. Even if you delete them, they can be found.

Above all, it is the name of Jesus that is at stake. We are followers of Jesus, and people are watching us. It's important that we rise above our own feelings, remember our actions matter, and above all honor one another and bring God glory.

THINK ABOUT IT

1. You just got fired. You didn't see it coming, and you don't think you deserved it. How do you respond? Write out your talking points for what you will say when asked about it.

2. Consider Proverbs 21:23: "Watch your words and hold your tongue; you'll save yourself a lot of grief" (MSG). When have you forgotten to apply this verse in a job situation, and how did it go?

PART THREE

BUILD A HEALTHY CULTURE

MANY YEARS AGO I WORKED FOR A SMALL ORGANIZATION that was effecting change on a national level. It was known for excellence, vision, and world-class leadership. It had a clear mission and strategy. With my acceptance into this organization came the respect of my friends and family for the achievement of such an honor.

But within a few months, I began to realize the department where I was placed did not represent the values of the overall organization. The leadership was more interested in saving face than making decisions based on integrity. Staff members talked about one another in highly negative terms. Complaining and whining were the most common modes of communication. There was little respect for the contribution of others on the team.

A friend and I tried to swing things back to a positive place, but we were sarcastically branded "Danny and Darla Do-Right" since we wouldn't participate in the negativity. Efforts to make central leadership aware of the toxic nature of the culture were directed back to department leadership—which, of course, was where the problems began. The department completely fractured toward the end of our assignment, and most team members left the organization hurt and disillusioned.

Richard Dore, the director of Proteus Leadership Centres, explained it this way:

> Having a great workplace culture can appear to be rare—and creating one is elusive and near impossible for some managers. People are often frustrated by their culture, with some describing their workplace as being dominated by negative and toxic personalities, with underhanded and manipulative infighting that stifles growth, innovation and results.[1]

There is nothing worse than working in an organization that has a bad culture. It doesn't matter how much money you make or how many weeks of vacation you are given; when you work in a toxic environment, you still come home tense and stressed at the end of each day. And that isn't worth it.

On the other hand, there is nothing better than working at an organization with a great culture. You wake up every day looking forward to getting back to work on the mission with people you enjoy being around.

What a Great Culture Looks Like

I'm sure this list isn't exhaustive, but here are twelve signs of a great culture in your organization, company, or church:

1. People are waiting in line to join your team. It's not because you are offering more money than they could find somewhere else. Many times the pay is less. But people have heard about your team, and they would give anything to be a part of it.

2. Turnover is low. You should especially pay attention to this in entry-level and mid-level jobs. Often top leaders will stay forever because it's safe and the pay is good. But if you see people staying for an unexpectedly long time in facility care, accounting, or children's ministry, you are probably looking at a healthy culture.

3. Top leaders are not insecure about other leaders succeeding. In fact, they encourage it. I've often been told how shocked people were that Mark Beeson, my senior leader at Granger, allowed multiple people on his staff to publish years before he ever did. That's because he built a culture where successes were celebrated at all levels.

4. Gossip isn't tolerated. It isn't just the leaders calling for people to take the high road in their communication. At every level, gossip is shut down with an encouragement to speak directly to the individual.

5. Lateral leadership is outstanding. Leading people below you is easy. That is, it's easy compared to leading people next to you over whom you have no authority. A great culture sees people coming alongside their peers to encourage, or occasionally to correct and redirect.

6. Team members are energized by the mission. You hear leaders at all levels of the organization talking about the mission. It gives them energy, and they are constantly thinking of ways to get it done.

7. It's not just a job; people *do life* together. They go to movies, hang out at one another's homes, and sometimes even vacation together. This doesn't mean they don't have other friends, but they really enjoy the company of the people they work with.

8. The team believes they are more important than the task. There is a sense that, as employees, they really matter. They

aren't just people filling tasks; but the culture, systems, language, and structure communicate value. Even in tough times with salary freezes or benefit changes, the vibe is still, "You matter!"

9. People are smiling. Walk the hallways and you will see people smiling, enjoying conversations, and having a good time in the midst of high productivity and intense focus.

10. Fear is missing. People don't fret if they say the wrong thing in front of the wrong person. There aren't hushed conversations because of the fear of what will happen if they are overheard. Employees in an organization with a great culture can walk into the boss's office with a concern and walk out knowing they were heard.

11. Communication is strong. From the top to the bottom, people communicate. The staff isn't surprised with information they didn't hear until it was announced at a Sunday service or came out in a new product brochure. It is communicated well in advance, with leaders even asking the staff to help find solutions.

12. Change is welcome. People aren't afraid of change. It's not that everyone likes change, but most have been through it so many times and have seen the leaders manage change with care and dignity that they no longer dread it.

Identifying the evidences of a great culture is all fine and good. But how do you go about creating such a culture?

I'm glad you asked. Keep reading.

CHAPTER TWENTY-SIX

TEAMS TRUMP PERSONALITY

IT WOULD BE A CRIME TO START A SEGMENT ABOUT BUILD-
ing a healthy culture without talking about teams. No organization,
church, government, or company can have a healthy culture and be
run by a dictator, monarch, or single personality.

John Maxwell said, "Teamwork is at the heart of great achievement. The question isn't whether teams have value. The question is
whether we acknowledge that fact and become better team players.
That's why I assert that *one is too small a number to achieve greatness.*
You cannot do anything of *real* value alone."[1]

Most executive leaders would say they have a team. But having a
team and operating as a team are two different things. Some would
say they have a team because they have multiple people on their
staffs. But it's quite possible, even normal, to have a multistaff organization with one person in charge and everyone else helping out.

Managers or department heads: Before you start pointing fin-
gers at your CEOs or lead pastors and calling them dictators, take
a look at your own area. Do you operate as a team? Or are you a
Mini-Me dictator barking orders and giving directions rather than
leaning on your team to help define direction and strategy?

I think I could count on one hand the organizations I know

that have a high-capacity, visionary, big-dog leader and that also operate as a team. It usually isn't the case.

Warning Signs of Poor Teamwork

If many of the following things are true in your organization, you can be certain teams will not thrive:

- Strong personalities dominate every discussion.
- People agree on something as a team only to see it reversed later by senior leadership.
- No one dares to "speak truth to power" and disagree with the senior leader.
- Debate is not encouraged.
- The group meets, but the top-dog leader rarely comes.
- The senior leader can't be in a meeting that he or she isn't leading.
- There is a revolving door for high-capacity leaders who report to the chief executive. They never stay on the team for long.
- People feel as though the leaders don't want input, or don't listen when they get it. Their minds are already made up.
- Leaders take individual credit for the accomplishments of the team.
- Change is not welcome unless the top-dog leader initiates it.
- After decisions are made, you'll hear comments such as, "I don't agree with it, but here is what was decided."
- When a decision or new direction is communicated, people walk away hearing the "what" but rarely understand the "why." There isn't broad ownership in the decision.
- When someone messes up, he or she is often left to hang on his or her own.

- There are lots of good discussions, but no one can remember what was decided at the last meeting, and people aren't held accountable for tasks.

———

Again, John Maxwell said, "Think of any highly effective leader, and you will find someone who surrounded himself with a strong inner circle. You can see it in business, ministry, sports, and even family relationships. Those closest to you determine your level of success."[2]

You can't have a healthy culture without a solid team at the helm. It is impossible.

THINK ABOUT IT

1. Does your organization have a true team model of leadership? If not, why not?

2. With your group, go through the list in this chapter and mark yes or no next to each characteristic, answering honestly whether or not it exists in your environment. Discuss every point that was marked with a yes.

CHAPTER TWENTY-SEVEN

THE THREE Ss

IF I WERE ONLY ALLOWED TO GIVE ONE REASON WHY THE organization where I served for twenty years was often described as having a healthy culture, it would certainly be a decision we made many years ago to meet together on a weekly basis.

You might be saying, "Uh, you have a staff meeting? Congratulations. Every organization has staff meetings." But this was different, and let me explain why.

This was a meeting we had every week that was for the distinct and single purpose of creating culture. We called it our weekly "SWAT" meeting—which is a cheesy acronym for "Staff Working As Team," but within this title is the purpose of the gathering.

This wasn't a meeting to make decisions; it was not a meeting to share prayer requests or worship (I know you think church leaders do this at every gathering); and it was not a meeting to fix things that were going wrong. None of those are bad, and they all help create culture to some degree. But instead, we focused solely on three areas we believed were the most effective at creating a healthy culture.

1. Stories

We spent the first fifteen to twenty minutes of every gathering sharing stories. We began the conversation by saying, "Where have you seen God at work in and through the church in the past seven days?" And then it was an open floor. We heard about changed lives inside and outside our walls. We heard stories from student ministry, small groups, and children's ministry. We found out about the person in Canada who wrote in after watching an online service. We heard about the experiences of people who attended for the first time, and the baptism of someone who had been away from church for decades. We learned about the woman who walked into the building lonely and afraid on a Monday afternoon, and who left having found encouragement and hope. We heard about the guy who was delivered a box of food in last year's food drive, and who came to help others receive food this year.

You can't underestimate the power of a story. It is so easy for people to get caught up in the micro-purpose of what they do: cleaning floors, organizing small groups, rehearsing lyrics, or preparing to teach kids. And sometimes you can work week after week and never see any tangible results from your work. But when you have an opportunity to gather every week and hear stories from your area and others, it does three things:

1. It keeps you from a silo mentality, or thinking you are the only one getting anything done.
2. It gives you a reason to celebrate what is happening all across the organization.
3. It gives you hope and reenergizes your vision when your team may be going through a tough season.

If I were running a company, I would do exactly the same thing. I would orient the story-telling segment of the meeting to share reports of great customer interactions or feedback. What are our customers saying? Where is our product helping better people's lives?

2. Spotlight

Following stories, we spent time putting one individual in the spotlight. With no warning ahead of time, we asked someone to sit up front and field questions from the rest of the team. We found out about his or her childhood, likes and dislikes, faith journey, spouse, hobbies, and history. This gave us an opportunity to get to know someone on a level we never did before. It took us out of the subculture of our individual departments, and it communicated that we were all on the same team, caring for one another as individuals.

Following the Q&A, we stopped and said, "Now let's tell [Jill] why we are so glad to have her on the team." And one after another we told her how her life added joy and meaning to the rest of us. People who were very close to her got to voice in front of others how significant she was to the team. The executive leaders got to communicate the value she brought to the entire organization. People who barely knew Jill got to tell her how they had been encouraged by her presence, smile, or attitude.

3. Stuff

The final segment in our meeting was used for sharing inside information. It added value to the team when they knew stuff ahead of time. Sometimes we talked about upcoming events; other times we were throwing concepts out that hadn't been decided on but that needed input from the team. They had ownership when they knew stuff before others, and it equipped them to answer questions and carry the vision.

Occasionally our "stuff" section consisted of one of the leaders talking about vision, teaching values, or sharing a spiritual lesson. These tended to be unprocessed thoughts. They felt more as if the leader was sharing off the top of his or her heart rather than delivering a prepared talk. Sometimes it was a bit raw, as it hadn't been written for a larger audience, but the staff really appreciated the authentic nature of being able to hear from their leaders as they were learning—not when it was all finished and packaged.

These weekly gatherings kept everyone on the team energized and focused. We realized, *It's not just about me or my department; I'm part of something bigger.* Even if we were having a tough week, for a few minutes we were pulled above that and realized again why it mattered. By the way, I would start this even if my business were brand-new with only one or two paid staff. And in the church setting, this would be fabulous to do regularly with a room full of volunteers.

So I'll say it again: if I were going to do one thing to create a positive culture, I would start with a weekly gathering and the three Ss. With our team at Granger, this ritual was hugely effective in keeping us focused in the same direction.

THINK ABOUT IT

1. What are you doing to intentionally create a healthy culture in your organization?

2. Do you have a weekly gathering where values and culture are experienced by your team? If not, what is stopping you from beginning such a meeting?

CHAPTER TWENTY-EIGHT

ALWAYS BELIEVE THE BEST

I HADN'T BEEN ON STAFF VERY LONG WHEN I FOUND AN e-mail written about me by someone on my team. It was a message sent between three individuals who were gossiping about me and suggesting I was involved in something that was deeply disturbing and wrong. It was full of ambiguous references and hearsay. As the e-mail string went along, the stories got more extreme, and the case against me was building in these individuals' minds. But it was utterly and completely false.

I was shocked. But more than that, I was hurt. I immediately took the e-mail chain to my boss and let him know of these accusations that were brewing. I offered to step down temporarily if needed so he could pursue the truth.

He didn't hesitate. He supported me 100 percent. He met with the three individuals and found they had zero evidence (except their own gossiping statements), and he quickly and sternly rebuked them for being involved in marring the reputation of a leader.

I was so surprised and honored that he had my back. When shots were aimed in my direction, he chose to stand by my side.

In order to have a healthy culture in your organization or business, you must believe the best about the others on your team. This is less about what you do and more about what you believe. It is less about strategy and more about a discipline of your mind.

- When people attack your team (and they will), always believe the best.
- When you receive an anonymous accusation about someone, throw it away. Why? Because you choose to always believe the best.
- When you hear one side of the story, and there is every reason to believe that your staff member's motives, intentions, or actions were wrong, wait. Don't react. Get the rest of the story. Believe the best.
- When there are two opposing sides, and it isn't clear what is true and what is false, always side with your team. Make the mental choice to believe the best about those who are standing by you and with you.

This isn't natural. It is easier to assume the worst. It's always easier to believe the gossip and fall for the slander. Sometimes it takes discipline and integrity to go against popular opinion. But your team will give their best, be at their best, and perform their best when they believe you have their backs.

When I was at Granger I received an e-mail that one of our pastors was having an affair with a woman in town. The anonymous note came from an address we didn't recognize and could not trace. I wrote back and told the person the only way I would listen to the accusation was if he or she would meet with me in person. The individual refused.

I wrote back and in the strongest words told this person that it was cowardly to make such an accusation against a leader while hiding behind anonymity. Because this person was accusing a pastor, I shared 1 Timothy 5:19, which says, "Do not entertain an accusation against an elder unless it is brought by two or three witnesses." And I proudly stood by the side of the accused.

If you receive an accusation with firsthand information, you are obligated to dive deeper.[1] But there is strength in believing the best in your team. If it's a "he says, she says" story without corroborating evidence, I'm going to believe the best of my team every time.

I'm a pretty secure leader. But nothing takes the wind out of my sails quicker than when I feel as if my leader does not trust me. If I know he or she loves me, trusts me, and has my back, then I can be the best at what God has wired me to do. That is true of most of us. Your team deserves your trust.

This doesn't mean you shouldn't deal with incompetence, bad attitudes, misaligned leaders, or the sinful choices of others. It also doesn't mean you should keep your head in the sand and not notice or deal with the obvious signs of trouble in the ranks. But those will be isolated situations. With most of your team most of the time, they need your undying loyalty and trust.

Whether they are below you, above you, or next to you in position, your team will soar if they know you have their backs.

THINK ABOUT IT

1. Have you ever been on the other side, with an untrue accusation thrown your direction, and felt the betrayal of others not believing the best about you? What was it like?

2. What do you do regularly to communicate to your team that you have their backs? What more can you do?

CHAPTER TWENTY-NINE
LET YOUR LEADERS LEAD

WE CALL IT THE LOOSE/TIGHT PRINCIPLE. THAT IS, YOU have to decide as a leader what you are going to hold on to loosely and what you are going to hold on to tightly.

For example, you likely want to hold on to your mission tightly. For most organizations, it's not up for debate. When you define your mission and communicate it over and over in many ways, it gives clarity to your direction. You likely have some major values and beliefs that are also tightly held.

On the other hand, there are a lot of things in the loose category. I love to bring great leaders on a team and then free them up to lead. They can make decisions, spend money, set direction, and develop initiatives—all without a huge approval process or a bunch of hoops to jump through to get permission.

In many organizations, problems emerge like this: Perhaps bad hiring decisions are made, so senior leaders jump in and start running things. Then the organization starts to get bottlenecked, and people get frustrated. High-capacity leaders begin to leave the organization. And the senior leader is too busy running things to properly interview potential replacements. So more bad hiring decisions are made. And the cycle continues.

If you want to develop a healthy culture, decide the nonnegotiables, bring great people on your team, then get out of the way and watch them do great things.

But even when you hire great people, there is another cycle that can take you down—and that also relates to running things with too heavy a hand. Perhaps you hire a great person. You take the time to ramp her up on values, vision, and the DNA of the organization. (So far, so good.) But then you give that leader responsibility without authority. You let her make all the micro-decisions, but hang on to the big decisions such as setting direction, approving expenditures, or making hiring decisions for her area. The high-capacity leader gets fed up and leaves your team. The leader isn't disloyal; she is just wired by God as a leader and a developer. And you won't let her do either. So now you have to start over looking for a great leader. You spend all your time looking for new staff and restating the values because you don't have any great leaders next to you to help.

Authority is the ability to make decisions without asking someone else's permission. So often we give a leader responsibility (e.g., run the youth ministry or oversee the marketing department) without also giving him the authority. The department leader has to get approval from the senior leader, or the person who says yes or no about expenses, or worse yet, a committee. Nothing frustrates a true leader more than not being able to make decisions, or than making decisions that are later reversed.

How to Free Your Leaders

If you want a great culture in which leaders are excited, then do six simple things:

1. Train them so their blood pulses with the mission, vision, and values of the organization.

2. Set them up to succeed. Lend them your credibility by telling everyone they are the leaders, and they have your full confidence.

3. Give them the authority to make decisions including spending money, hiring and firing staff, and setting direction for their areas.

4. Get out of the way and let them lead.

5. Connect with them continually for evaluation, values review, and rare course corrections. Be available as a sounding board to process decisions. Remember, they don't need you to tell them the answer. Rather, they need you to ask questions and help them process the right course of action.

6. Celebrate their wins publicly, and reward them with greater responsibility as appropriate.

This is easy to put on a list, but much harder to practice. Find a leader you know who is great at empowering and releasing other leaders—and watch him or her closely. Within that leader you will likely find someone who is great at producing a healthy culture.

THINK ABOUT IT

1. Make a list of what is held tightly or loosely in your organization. Are the loose things really loose, or do you sometimes swoop in and micromanage?

2. Do you have leaders to whom you've given responsibility without authority? What can you do to clarify their roles?

CHAPTER THIRTY

HAVE FUN

A FRIEND TOLD ME RECENTLY HE OVERHEARD A COWORKER saying, "Just because we work together doesn't mean I have to like you." Really? How can we be pulling together, working for the same vision, and attempting to achieve the same goals if we are only tolerating one another's presence? And do we think our customers or church members are automatons and won't pick up on the tension?

When you work at a church, it isn't just a job. It's not just about fulfilling a responsibility. It is also about doing life together. It is about being the church while you are leading the church. It is about having fun, working through conflict, accomplishing ministry, and yes, being highly effective in your job.

When you are a Christian leader working in business, it also isn't just about a job. Your life is the only Jesus some people will ever see. It's important that you model God's love for those around you, whether they recognize it as such or not. You are in a unique position to help people find meaning in their work, and creating opportunities for fun can do just that.

At Granger, we valued chemistry and affinity as highly as—if not higher than—education, skills, experience, and passion (refer back to chapter 14). And that is why we intentionally planned time to have fun. In the old days, when our staff was much smaller, we would all jump in our vehicles and go to a movie, or out to eat, or miniature golfing. As the staff size increased, much of that happened in a decentralized fashion.

For example, our communications team headed to a nearby town for an IMAX movie, our children's team experienced a high ropes course together, and the arts staff gathered for a family pool party and cookout.

The affinity doesn't grow on its own. It must be nurtured with intentionality. It is worth an investment of time and money on "fun" to build a culture where your staff is energized and committed to one another for the long term.

Strategic Fun

To make this a reality, several things have to be true:

- Priority. Although fun doesn't require much money, you have to make fun a priority in your budget. It won't just happen.
- Accessibility. This can't be something that just senior leadership does. If so, it's an executive perk rather than a strategic part of shaping culture.
- Modeling. At the same time, you have to demonstrate fun. One of my leaders thanked me for valuing fun and downtime during our senior team gatherings because it gave her permission and encouragement to do the same in her department.
- Inclusiveness. Even with a large staff, do a couple of things each year with the entire team. My wife and I always hosted a summer picnic, and at Christmas our team put on a formal dinner for everyone and their spouses.

- Just do it. You can't wait for the work to get done to experience fun. For some of your staff, you'll need to tell them this is "required fun." Otherwise they will never participate either because (a) they don't have a felt need for fun, or (b) they think they have too much to do.

Doug Smoker is a friend who owns and operates Smoker Craft. His family has been making boats for five generations, and last summer they made the local news when they created a fun opportunity for their staff. The local station reported:

> More than 1,000 people got into the Elkhart County 4-H Fair free Friday, thanks to a New Paris boat company. Smoker Craft invited all of its roughly 300 employees out for a night of family fun. Each worker was allowed to bring up to ten family members. It was part of their annual "Family Reunion," but this is the first year the company held the event at the fair. They provided food, drinks and ride wristbands for kids.[1]

What an amazing story for our community. I'm sure those employees felt incredibly valued as the leaders made this a priority with their time and budget.

A couple of years ago the church where I worked rented an entire theater on the release date for *The Hobbit* so our staff and their families could experience it together. Sure, it cost a lot of money in a season when we had cut our budget six times since it had last increased. But I believe the little bit of money you invest in creating a great culture now will save you a hundredfold later.

THINK ABOUT IT

1. What have you intentionally planned for your team in the fun category?

2. Do your leaders know it is okay to occasionally plan fun activities for their teams? If not, what will you do to change this?

CHAPTER THIRTY-ONE

MEETINGS THAT WORK

Facebook status update: "Long day with lots of meetings."
Comment #1: "I'm so sorry!"
Comment #2: "Where can I send a sympathy card?"
Comment #3: "Just kill yourself and get it over with—ha!"
Comment #4: "Boooooorrrrrrriiiiinnnnngggg"
Comment #5: "Hope you were able to play Angry Birds to pass the time."

THESE RESPONSES AREN'T TOO UNCOMMON, ARE THEY? IT seems as if there is a general disdain of meetings.

But that's not how I look at meetings. I often find meetings to be the most productive moments of my week. It is a time I can connect with people I enjoy, talk about things I'm passionate about, and make progress that will have real impact on real people.

But I've also been in many meetings that couldn't end soon enough. Sometimes it was because the leader wasn't prepared, or the wrong people were in the room, or no one was clear about why we were meeting.

Keys to Productive Meetings

Here are some things I've found helpful in making sure meetings stay useful—and relatively painless—for everyone:

BREATHING ROOM

Don't overpack your agenda, and don't underestimate the importance of relational connection time. While you shouldn't chase down every topic that is spontaneously brought up in the meeting, healthy teams allow meetings to be sidetracked on occasion. Sometimes the highest priority of the moment is experiencing community.

CLEAR GAME PLAN

The most productive meetings happen when you know who is leading the meeting and what you are planning to accomplish by the time you adjourn. Write your goal(s) for the meeting on the top of the agenda. For a thirteen-hour, senior team meeting (two full days) I held at Granger, I published the goals at the beginning of the first day. None of us thought we'd be able to accomplish them within two days. Yet by keeping the goals in front of us and reviewing them every few hours, we kept focused, avoided rabbit-trail conversations, and accomplished every single goal by the end of the second day.

OPEN-FORUM AGENDA

When possible, send the agenda out ahead of time. Give people a chance to contribute. If they don't give you something for the agenda before the meeting, then you should rarely let them bring it up during the meeting. Just say, "That's a great topic. Let's discuss it off-line and consider adding it to next week's agenda." That said, don't put everything on the agenda that is submitted. Some items really aren't worth the time for the entire group to discuss. Get used to saying, "Let's discuss that off-line," or "You should get with Jane and Bob and come back with a recommendation."

ACTION POINTS

End the meeting with a "*who* will do *what* by *when*" list and distribute this immediately following the meeting. Use this printed list to start your next meeting.

STACKED MEETING DAYS

Consider stacking your meetings. I tried to stack all my meetings on Tuesdays and Wednesdays. When I arrived on those days, I knew it was a meeting day. I didn't have to fret that I was not getting my to-do list done. Likewise, on Mondays or Fridays I could be a productivity machine since I had very few meetings. And make sure to prioritize. Put the big rocks in first. Make sure your most important meetings are given priority on your schedule, and if other small-pebble meetings can fit around the big rocks, great. But if not, don't schedule them.

RUN WITH IT

If you find a meeting to be a waste of time, yet you aren't the leader, then start leading up. I've been in that situation many times and have asked permission to come alongside a positional leader to help with preparing for the meeting, establishing the agenda, or running point to keep the meeting productive. Likewise, if you are running the meeting for your boss, be sure to get his or her input in advance of the meeting to make sure your boss's concerns are scheduled for discussion.

Ground Rules

In 2006, I attended the Drive Conference at North Point Community Church in Alpharetta, Georgia.[1] Andy Stanley shared some great thoughts on leading meetings:

- Pull members into the discussion.
- Don't interrupt a debate—listen. Some of you are peacemakers and try to smooth everything over. This doesn't help. Fan the flame of conflict. If you have great leaders on your team, they will be highly opinionated and very persuasive. You need to have an environment where things can be debated and you are fine with it.
- Don't attempt to resolve tension—it won't really be resolved.
- Don't allow team members to interrupt each other.
- When you sense someone isn't listening but only waiting to talk, address it.
- Keep the discussion focused.
- When a sensitive subject is going to be discussed, give those who may feel threatened a heads-up.[2]

Here is the bottom line: if you are in a culture where meetings feel like a waste of time, change the culture. How? One meeting at a time.

THINK ABOUT IT

1. You probably can't control or fix every meeting in your organization, but what is one regular meeting you can immediately address?

2. Is there a leader you should come alongside and tell, "Let me run point on these meetings for you"? What's the best way to do that?

CHAPTER THIRTY-TWO

LISTEN TO YOUR TEAM

DAN WIEDEN IS AN ADVERTISING LEGEND AND COFOUNDER of Wieden + Kennedy. His leadership style is unpacked in the book *Mavericks at Work* by authors William C. Taylor and Polly LaBarre.[1] I find his example refreshing and uncharacteristically humble for a leader of a huge organization with more than six hundred staff.

Wieden argued that his job is to "walk in stupid every day"— to keep challenging the organization, and himself, to seek out unexpected ideas, outside influences, and new perspectives on old problems.

"It's the hardest thing to do as a leader," said Wieden, "but it's the most important thing. Whatever day it is, something in the world has changed overnight, and you better figure out what it is and what it means. You have to forget what you did and what you just learned. You have to walk in stupid every day."[2]

Unfortunately, too many leaders walk in every day as if they are the experts. Either because of their positions, tenures, or influences, they act as if they no longer have anything to learn from others (and especially not from the people they hired). They don't attend conferences, they never ask questions in an effort to learn, and they only read books or listen to podcasts when they are preparing for their next talks.

Authors Taylor and LaBarre continued,

> It's hard to find an executive who doesn't appreciate the power of the experience curve—the idea that the more you do something . . . the more productive you become. Dan Wieden and his colleagues also appreciate the power of the inexperience curve—the idea that the more you do something, the more important it is to challenge the assumptions and habits that built your success so as to generate a wave of innovations to build the future.[3]

Interpretation: Just because your church or company is growing, don't get cocky. Don't stop listening. Don't stop asking questions. Don't keep doing what you did yesterday just because it worked. Don't surround yourself with a bunch of people who check their brains at the door. Don't ignore people who challenge your insecurities as a leader—yes, we all have them. Walk in stupid, and you might learn something.

It is all about listening. There is nothing that will empower and encourage your team more than to know you listen to them. John Maxwell said, "The greatest enemy of learning is knowing." [4]

Authors Chip Heath and Dan Heath put it this way: "Once we know something, we find it hard to imagine what it was like not to know it. Our knowledge has 'cursed' us."[5] Those who know stuff walk around as if they know stuff rather than walking around wanting to learn. And no one wants to work for a know-it-all. It pulls down the culture you are trying to lift.

I recently read some good leadership advice coming from Bryan

Singer, director of the movie *Superman Returns*. In *Fast Company* magazine, he talked about the importance of consulting with his creative team and listening to them. He said, "I surround myself with people who understand me and aren't afraid to tell me when I'm straying. They're not sycophants, they're friends."[6]

Are You a Learner?

A secure leader, one who listens to learn, creates a culture that is attractive and collaborative. John Maxwell offered these ten questions to self-assess whether you are a learner:

1. Am I open to other people's ideas?
2. Do I listen more than I talk?
3. Am I open to changing my opinion based on new information?
4. Do I readily admit when I am wrong?
5. Do I observe before acting on a situation?
6. Do I ask questions?
7. Am I willing to ask a question that will expose my ignorance?
8. Am I open to doing things in a way I haven't done before?
9. Am I willing to ask for directions?
10. Do I act defensive when criticized, or do I listen openly for truth?[7]

This is one area of building a healthy culture that might require a dose of humility and some new skills. If you *think* you *might* need help learning how to listen, I guarantee your team knows you do.

THINK ABOUT IT

1. Answer the previous ten questions honestly. Then ask your spouse or close coworker to also assess you on the same questions. Discuss where you differ.

2. If you struggle with listening, develop the discipline of asking three questions before you begin talking about yourself or sharing your knowledge.

CHAPTER THIRTY-THREE
ASK QUESTIONS

ASKING QUESTIONS MAY BE ONE OF THE LEAST TALKED about secret weapons of a great leader. In fact, I believe it may be one of the most undeveloped skills in leadership. Many businesses and nearly all churches are filled with leaders who are professional communicators. That is, they are paid to talk. They spend a good portion of their time figuring out what they are going to say and how they are going to say it, and then delivering the message.

They don't get hired to ask people questions. They get hired to tell people what they think or believe about a certain topic or product. Pastors are the worst offenders—they are so used to everyone wanting to hear what they have to say that they have a difficult time listening to (or caring about) what others have to say.

Yet the Bible we carry around and teach from is very clear:

Everyone should be quick to listen, slow to speak. (James 1:19)

Spouting off before listening to the facts is both shameful and foolish. (Prov. 18:13 NLT)

As author and management consultant Peter Drucker put it, "The leader of the past was a person who knew how to tell. The leader of the future will be a person who knows how to ask."[1]

Back in the day, it was possible for one person to hold most of the knowledge and be able to guide an organization to success through working the system. Not anymore. Today's world is moving too fast, information is changing too rapidly, and no one person (or group of people) has an edge on what is needed for success.

Additionally, a person who doesn't ask questions comes off as proud and untouchable. There is an air of superiority that emanates from the know-it-all. He or she may not know it, but others don't enjoy being around someone who has all the answers.

A person who asks questions

- assumes there is something she can learn;
- exudes humility;
- infuses confidence in people around him;
- helps introverts or nonverbal leaders communicate; and
- is constantly learning.

A person who doesn't ask questions

- assumes she already knows all the facts;
- exudes a cocky attitude;
- risks looking like a fool;
- shuts down people who don't have as forceful of a personality;
- impresses himself more than others; and
- forfeits prime learning opportunities.

Just Ask Leadership

I had the opportunity to interview author Gary Cohen about his book *Just Ask Leadership*.[2] So much of what he wrote connects with my thoughts about leadership. Here are some notable takeaways from the book, and from my conversation with Gary:

- Hold back. In meetings, leaders have difficulty keeping quiet when they have an idea that's better than the ones currently being batted around. Revealing that idea, however, often spoils the learning and discovery process of their coworkers.
- Rein it in. If you think you're talking too much in a meeting, so does everyone else.
- Individualize. Centralized leadership doesn't work with the current generation. People want to work their way, not your way. They know what motivates them and how they best achieve results and obtain information, and they want to receive full credit for their efforts.
- Get it from the source. The person best equipped to solve a problem is the one who lives with it every day.

Not long ago I was in an all-day meeting with several coworkers. We had brought in a consultant from across the country to help guide our conversations and lead us to some significant decisions. I was sitting next to a leader and noticed he was multitasking all day long. He would answer e-mails, work on projects, and also jump in and out of participating in the meeting.

It annoyed me a bit. We spent a lot of money to make this meeting happen, and I needed the best of what he could bring. I could have jumped on him during a break and told him to turn his e-mail off. I could have made a general announcement to everyone to focus and turn off outside distractions. I could have sent him a scolding e-mail the next day.

Instead, I waited for a full week. The next time we met together for our weekly face time, I asked a few questions. It went something like this: "Last week I couldn't help but notice you were answering e-mails and working on projects during our meeting. Tell me about that. Did you find it difficult to focus on the topic? Was the day's discussion boring to you? Is there something I've done to communicate that your wisdom and participation in those discussions isn't welcome? Is there something we can do to change the environment?"

He came back to me a few days later and thanked me for the way I approached it. He felt honored and respected. This is just one example of hundreds I've experienced where asking questions, rather than drawing conclusions and making statements, has been the key to removing emotion and finding a solution to a problem.

———

When we were trying to discover the five-year vision for Granger, we took the unprecedented step of going to every single person in the church and asking him or her to help us. We didn't want to come off the mountaintop like Moses with a word from God and say, "Here is the five-year vision. Read it and weep!" Rather, we wanted to give every single person in the church an opportunity to participate. So we asked questions like these:

- If this church could be everything you wanted in five years for your family, what would that look like?
- If this church was exactly the type of church to help you reach your friends who don't currently attend, what would it look like?

- If this church was transforming our entire community and making our city a better place to live, what would we be doing differently?

And it was an amazing discovery process.[3] There were key parts of the five-year vision that we constructed by asking questions. And the questions weren't a disguised way to find people who would agree with what we were already planning. Rather, the vision came from the answers we got from asking the right questions.

Authenticity is key. You can ask questions in order to manipulate people to do what you want and make them think it was their idea. But that's not authentic, question-based leadership. That might get you what you want. But you risk losing credibility in the process. Gary Cohen said it this way:

> The right questions rely on the leader's ability to communicate authentic interest in learning the answer. They come from a place of not knowing. The right questions are open-ended, carry the possibility of true discovery, and demonstrate a willingness to share and bestow credit.[4]

THINK ABOUT IT

1. Why do you think business professionals like Peter Drucker and Gary Cohen are advocating for a style of leadership that comes straight from Scripture and exemplifies the humility of a Christ-follower?

2. What do you need to change about your leadership so that you talk less and listen more?

CHAPTER THIRTY-FOUR

DEALING WITH MISTAKES

WHAT DO YOU DO WHEN SOMEONE MAKES A MISTAKE? I WAS talking with a coworker about a decision he made as he wondered, "Did I just cost the church three hundred dollars by giving the wrong answer?"

No, he didn't, but it reminded me of mistakes I've made over the years. Some haven't cost anything; others have been very expensive. At one of my first jobs, I was responsible for mowing a large property. Laverne, the maintenance supervisor, showed me how to use the tractor. "Does everything make sense?" he asked as he finished his training.

"Yep, I've got it." As he walked away, I put the tractor in gear and proceeded to drive it directly into the side of the building and through a closed garage door.

Sometimes mistakes aren't really mistakes. They are just decisions that are made with the best information available, but later the information is proven to be faulty. For example, in 1995 I made the decision to accept a design from an architect for an artistic pattern on the side of a brick wall. We were certain it would be a temporary wall. However, it was ugly the day it went up, and we had to look at it for sixteen long years before it was removed. Every day for sixteen years I was reminded of this bad decision.

What do you do when someone who reports to you makes a mistake? You could say to yourself, *He made a mistake. It cost the company money. He is going to pay for it.* Perhaps you would make him or her financially reimburse the company. Or you might try the humiliation route. A couple of years ago, when I went to our local Taco Bell, I noticed everyone had matching uniforms and hats, except one guy who was wearing a fluorescent pink hat. When he turned around, I saw the words on the front: "I forgot my hat today." I'm sure his boss thought he was teaching him a lesson (yeah, find a different boss).

Another option is to consider the mistake part of your training budget. Tom Watson, the founder of IBM, understood the value of mistakes. Once, one of his employees made a huge mistake that cost the company millions of dollars. The employee, upon being called into his office, said, "I suppose you want my resignation."

"Are you kidding?" replied Watson. "I just spent ten million dollars educating you."[1]

In the church world, our mistakes are not typically that large. But it isn't too uncommon for leaders to get bent out of shape when a mistake is made that costs the church money. It comes from a well-intentioned place of wanting to be wise stewards of the church resources. But it diminishes people and discourages innovation and appropriate risk.

When Laverne looked at me after I drove the tractor through the side of the building and said, "I'm guessing you won't do that again," he was right—although I did drive it through a glass window a couple of days later. But what I remember most about that day was his graceful posture on helping me grow through my mistake.

Now, if someone keeps making the same mistake over and over, then it is obvious the education process isn't working. Release him or her to spend someone else's money making mistakes.

I've worked for two employers over the past twenty-nine years since I graduated high school, and I'm grateful that in both places I have been encouraged to risk, inspired to innovate, and given room to fail. It has cost those organizations a few bucks, but it has made me a much better leader—which ultimately made the organizations better.

THINK ABOUT IT

1. Have you been too unforgiving when people under you make mistakes? Has someone been unforgiving of you? What are the consequences?

2. What should you change about your leadership style to encourage innovation and risk, even if you know it will open room for mistakes?

CHAPTER THIRTY-FIVE

ALL IN

WAY BACK WHEN I WAS FIRST HIRED AT GRANGER, MY BOSS talked about the importance of attending the church where you work. At first I thought he was joking—I had never heard of anyone working at a church where he or she did not attend. He told me of several situations where that was unfortunately true.

I wrongly assumed it was a dying pattern. In fact, the number of churches I hear about who hire staff members to do jobs rather than ministry is increasing. Recently I learned of a large church that had a senior-level staff member who attended a different church. He sat on the leadership team, making decisions about starting and stopping ministry programs at a church he did not even attend. I learned of another church where staff members in the accounting department were prohibited from attending the church. I know of another church with a preschool where the teachers do not attend the church, and in fact, they are known to speak negatively to the parents about the church.

I think I know where this comes from. Pastors have been burned, and so they make policies to reduce potential conflict. Somewhere along the way they had to fire someone, and that person left the church in a huff with all his or her friends and family members. And so they said, "Never again." They figured it would be easier to manage conflict if the individual didn't get rooted in the church.

I get it. When I had to let employees go, they often left the church angry and confused. Which meant all their family members who attended left too. And their best friends. And a few people who just started attending who heard about the drama and decided they didn't want to get involved. And honestly, on those dark days I wondered about changing my philosophy.

But I decided I would much rather deal with potential conflict than have staff members who were just doing a job. I wanted every person on staff to care about the people of the church as much as I did. I wanted to "do life" with those on staff, walking with them through the ups and downs of life, knowing there were people around them to love them, challenge them, and encourage them. I wanted staff members who handled the money, took care of the facility, led the kids, and made the decisions to do so with high integrity because it was not *only* their employer, it was also the place where they worship.

It would be easy to slip on this conviction. Just before I left Granger, we opened an early learning center. It would have been an easy decision to let it run as a business within our walls. With about a dozen hires in the plan, the case could have been made to hire the best educators in town, regardless of their church affiliations or faith walks. But we made the decision for this to be a high-quality learning center that is faith based and highly integrated with the ministries of our church. We didn't want it to be a business that shares space. We wanted teachers who are ministers and who love the church.

If you are trying to create a positive culture that is unified in vision and purpose, you want people on your team who are all in—100 percent. Nothing held back.

THINK ABOUT IT

1. Do you have any policies that have been written because of hurts from the past? Should these be reconsidered?

2. Do you have people on your team who only attend the church because they have to as a condition of employment? Consider a conversation with them.

CHAPTER THIRTY-SIX

LEADERSHIP RETREATS

SCHEDULING A WEEK AWAY FOR YOUR LEAD TEAM TO PLAN, strategize, pray, and focus is not only smart, it's an absolute must for a growing organization that wants to build a healthy culture.

A retreat for your leaders does two things:

1. It allows them to get away from the tyranny of the urgent and fly high for several days. From this vantage point, you can identify bottlenecks and make strategic decisions that will guide your next season of business or ministry.
2. It gives others in the organization a confidence that their leaders are taking the time to make solid decisions. It also models the practice of getting out of the busyness, clearing your mind, and determining the right next steps. This helps build a healthier culture.

Based on my experience, here is some advice for your next leadership retreat:

Planning

- Plan an agenda, but don't be too tied to your agenda.
- Leave room for fun.
- Consider inviting the spouses to come along.
- Get it on the calendar months in advance.
- Don't wait until you feel a need for a retreat—by that time it is too late.
- Don't think you have to spend lots of money. Pastors: Ask families in your church if anyone has an empty vacation home, an unused timeshare, or accumulated miles for flights.

Discussions: Getting Down to Business

- Before you begin, agree on outcomes. For example, for this retreat to be successful, we need to accomplish

  _____.

- Don't get sidetracked on micro-issues; focus on macro-issues.
- Someone should be responsible for keeping the agenda moving. This decision isn't a matter of position (who is in charge?) but more of a skill-based choice (who is best suited to keep us focused?).
- Make sure you are having fun.
- Ask big questions to get people thinking and talking. When reflecting on big issues such as "What is our mission?" start by having everyone take a stab at it alone. Then come together, compare notes, and figure out what you agree on and what needs lots of conversation.
- Bring a Post-it easel pad. Use the sheets to brainstorm and stick them around the room for reference.

- Consider bringing someone in from the outside to help facilitate conversations. But have him or her stay somewhere else so your team can be relaxed during the downtime.
- When initiating change, make an APA list. Put three columns on the board. On the left column, write everything you want to *Avoid* when you make this change. In the middle column, write everything you want to *Preserve*. And in the right column, write everything you want to *Achieve* through this change.
- For the big discussions, ask everyone to turn off his or her phone notifications and e-mails. People cannot multitask as well as they think they can, and you need 110 percent from everyone when you are making big decisions about strategy and direction.

Downtime

- Eat lots of meals together.
- If possible, stay together. For example, rather than individual hotel rooms, rent a house or stay in a lodge together.
- Pray together.
- Are we having fun yet?
- Schedule relaxation and social time. And don't feel guilty about spending money to make that happen. Your organization needs a leadership team that loves doing life together. Those fun times on retreats will sustain you when you are back in the saddle and ministry is hard.
- Don't throw the retreat in the faces of those who are not there by tweeting pictures or reporting every minute on Facebook.

Reflection

- Summarize results. What did we decide? Where do we have consensus? What needs more discussion?
- Make a "*who* will do *what* by *when*" list. Go through this list during your normal weekly meetings following the retreat.

————

I have held leadership retreats as close as a cabin a few miles away, and as far away as a donated house in Mexico. The location isn't as important as the discipline of the annual schedule. Make a commitment to do this, and you will be amazed by how God provides for the details and the budget.

THINK ABOUT IT

1. Do you not have a leadership retreat on the schedule? What is keeping you from getting it on the schedule?

2. Does your senior leader normally lead these types of meetings? Is he or she best suited to drive an agenda? If not, identify the person who can best facilitate your annual retreats and weekly meetings.

CHAPTER THIRTY-SEVEN

HOURS AND FLEXIBILITY

I WORK WITH A LOT OF EXECUTIVE PASTORS, AND A RECUR-ring question goes something like this: "How many hours should I require my staff to work?" A follow-up question is often, "Should I make everyone work the same hours?"[1]

Let me address this in two parts, the first related to you as the leader, and the second focused on your employees.

The Leader's Hours

In ministry it is difficult to differentiate working hours from non-working hours. Almost everything you do is related to ministry, so when are you not working? You get a call at home that turns into a forty-five-minute counseling session; you visit a member at the hospital on a Saturday afternoon; you work on your presentation late into the night at home. It's not that different for those who work in business in an executive or management role. You answer e-mails on your off hours, you make phone calls in the evening to that associate who is in a different time zone, and at times you probably travel over the weekends.

So even though it is difficult to differentiate hours, I think it is incredibly important to disengage, to find out what renews you, and to spend time with people you love hanging out with.

I had a boss who often said, "There are three parts to every day. You should work really hard for two of them, and take the third one off." That's not always practical, of course, and we tend to work in spurts. We sprint for a while, then rest, then sprint, then rest. That's okay, as long as you are resting adequately between the sprints. But the essence of this axiom is right on: make sure you aren't working 24-7.

This also has to do with your phase of life. Years ago I didn't have four little ones at home, and I could work a sixty-hour week and still be balanced at home. Today that isn't true. In order to be a leader of integrity, I have to lead as well at home and in my personal relationships as I do in my professional role. That means I'm rushing from the office to cross-country meets or marching-band competitions a couple of times a week during the school year.

Pay attention to your body. Don't let your emotional, physical, or spiritual tanks run dry. Get people around you who can wave the red flag before you go too far down the out-of-balance path.

The Employees' Hours

At the church where I worked we had some positions that required specific hours. These would include facility care staff who worked on shifts, preschool teachers who needed to be there for the kids at certain times, and restaurant employees who also had set hours.

However, most of our staff positions were more flexible. And that was intentional. In today's world, more people value flexibility in their schedules than they do compensation, extra benefits, or more vacation time.

This is especially true of the younger people on your staff.

Marketing firm Euro RSCG Worldwide[2] reported recently on a *Time* magazine website that generation Y employees (those born between 1982 and 1993) are rejecting the traditional eight-hour workday.[3]

The following observations were among their findings:

- Gen Y workers won't accept jobs where they can't access Facebook.
- Gen Y workers value workplace flexibility over more money.
- Gen Y workers are always connected to jobs through technology.[4]

In talking about companies that are hesitant to adopt flexible work arrangements, they said, "Many companies fear that, without structure, employees will be distracted, not as engaged and less productive. In fact, the opposite is often true. A trusting work environment breeds more-loyal employees and increases efficiency."[5]

The old command-and-control type of leadership will find it increasingly difficult to retain a growing workforce that desires flexibility. And it's not just Gen Y staff: I had several working moms on my team who valued the flexibility I gave them on non-school days to juggle their schedules around to accommodate their mom duties.

Leading Flexibly

A healthy culture is built with some flexibility in the system. That doesn't mean it is a free-for-all structure or schedule. There are still expectations and responsibilities, and each department supervisor is responsible for how flexibly his or her team can function.

Keep in mind:

- If you have slackers on your team, you may need to provide some structure and hold them accountable to it.[6] A true slacker has a character problem, and this can rarely be fixed, so you may need to require that person to follow a specific schedule just so you have a good excuse to fire him or her. However, be careful not to categorize everyone as a slacker who doesn't meet your expectations.

- Ask, "Are they getting their jobs done satisfactorily?" rather than, "Were they at their desks for a certain number of hours?"

- You may want to determine certain all-in times, when everyone is present. For example, we had a team full of creatives, so very little of what they did was structured. However, twice each week they had a required fifteen-minute meeting to touch base, gather information, and connect on projects.

- There may be certain seasons when a boss wants things to be less flexible. For example, in a recent overhaul of a certain department, we required all staff to be in the office for the same eight hours on Tuesday, Wednesday, and Thursday. This allowed us to rebuild the relational core and strategic unity of the team while still giving them flexibility on the other days of the week.

- Ignore the urge to block Twitter or Facebook from your office environment. People's lives are much more integrated now than ever. They may shoot off a private message to a friend on Facebook during the day, but they will also stay remotely connected and work on office projects at night or on the weekends. If you have someone who is excessive in his or her time online, deal with that person individually. But don't disconnect your staff from one of the best ways to stay connected to your members or customers.

I know this idea of high flexibility goes against the grain of many leaders. It is much more difficult to track and control. But organizations with great cultures and high employee satisfaction always have found a way to release flexibility while increasing productivity.

THINK ABOUT IT

1. Are you unsure if your structure is too inflexible? Survey your staff and ask them to rank what would be most important to them (e.g., more money, more flexible hours, better office, tools, or benefits).

2. Are you personally maintaining a good work–life balance? Would your spouse agree?

CHAPTER THIRTY-EIGHT

FAIRNESS IS OVERRATED

IT'S ONE OF THE MOST OFTEN REPEATED PHRASES A PARent hears for the first eight or ten years of a kid's life: "That's not fair!" As parents, we become arbiters of spats over toys, time, who goes first, how the food is divided, who has to go to bed first, whose turn it is on the video game, and a hundred other daily disputes over fairness. We try to walk the line of making sure our little kids aren't being bullied or mistreated by the older kids, while at the same time teaching them life lessons such as *life isn't fair.*

When it comes to the business or church world, as leaders we should not make fairness a priority. That sounds harsh, doesn't it? In an age of political correctness and tolerance, it seems wrong to admit that some things aren't fair. But fairness is overrated.

- In the church, we aren't fair about what gets promotion or marketing space. Some departments or upcoming events get priority.
- We aren't fair about which events get facility space.
- Jesus wasn't fair when he chose to spend most of his time with his twelve disciples. Furthermore, he wasn't fair when he chose three disciples above the rest of them.

- As a leader, I'm not fair with my time. Some people can call and get time with me at a moment's notice. Other people can't. That's not fair.
- We aren't fair when we determine what gets put into the budget and what doesn't.
- I'm not fair with my influence. I focus a great deal of my influence with some people, and none at all with other people.
- We aren't fair with our compensation. Through a fairness filter, it may appear that two people have the same position, have been on staff the same amount of time, and have the same education and expertise. Yet because of capacity, potential, replacement cost, or the value they add to our company, their salaries might be different.

We make decisions based on priority, not fairness. We filter discussions through our mission and values, not whether it is fair. We determine budget dollars and facility requests through our purposes, not whether someone will get his or her feelings hurt.

If you think through your own choices, I would guess you aren't fair either. For example, I'm not fair with the time I spend with women. My wife gets a disproportionate percentage of my time. I do not apologize for that. I do not try to balance or give other women equal time.

Also, there are four kids on this planet with whom I spend more time than any other kids. They are Heather, Megan, Hunter, and Taylor Stevens. It isn't fair that I don't spend as much time with Tommy or Ashley or Jake—but I don't care. Because they aren't my children. I'll be nice to them, and they can come by the house anytime—but I'm going to unfairly spend most of my time with my kids.

Don't confuse fairness with justice. Justice is about doing what is right. Fairness means everyone gets exactly the same thing.

Remember the story from the Bible we talked about in chapter 23? A businessman hired a group of laborers to work in his field at 9:00 a.m. They negotiated and agreed upon a price. This same businessman hired workers again at noon, 3:00 p.m., and 6:00 p.m. Each time he offered them a wage and they agreed. At the end of the day, the workers hired first saw that those hired throughout the day were getting the same amount of money, even though they worked for fewer hours.

Was that fair? Not at all. Fairness would have dictated the same hourly rate. It was not fair, but it was just. They all got exactly what they agreed to. And it was up to the businessman to decide. No one was mistreated.

Don't apologize for not being fair. However, don't stretch this principle to discrimination. If someone is denied time, attention, promotion, or pay because of his or her skin color or gender, that is discrimination—and that is not just *or* fair. And as Christian leaders, we should stand against it.

THINK ABOUT IT

1. Where have you tried to be fair in order to keep people happy when a decision needed to be made regardless of fairness?

2. Where have you been unfair (bordering on discrimination) because of a person's ethnicity, gender, or life phase?

CHAPTER THIRTY-NINE

IDENTIFY SILOS

VERY LITTLE WILL TEAR AT THE HEALTHY CULTURE YOU ARE trying to build more than departmental silos. These exist in just about every corporation and organization. If you have more than one department in your church, you are susceptible to silos. Even small businesses experience silos, between servers and busboys or between product development and marketing.

Silos are the walls that are between departments in an organization. Business author Patrick Lencioni wrote about the concept of silos, or unhealthy divisions: "Silos rise up not because of what executives are doing purposefully but rather because of what they are failing to do: provide themselves and their employees with a compelling context for working together."[1]

Silos turn colleagues into competitors. For a business, *Forbes* contributor John Kotter said, "A siloed organization cannot act quickly on opportunities that arise in a fast-paced business landscape, nor is it able to make productive decisions about how to change in order to seize these opportunities."[2]

For a church, the stakes are even higher. Silos will tear apart a church faster than just about anything. From a silo-built church come jealousy, slander, gossip, bitterness, conflict, and competition.

Your attendees are smart, and they can sniff this stuff out pretty quickly. They experience jealous competition in their homes and in their workplaces—if they find it at church, they either won't sign up or won't stay.

But here is the problem: the natural order of the universe in your organization is for silos to be built and turf-guarding to happen. It just happens. You have to try extremely hard to destroy the silos. It is rare to find churches or businesses that don't have silos, and it's not because they are lucky or fortunate. They have worked like crazy to keep silos from developing. It requires difficult communication, strong leadership, and people who are more concerned about the overall mission than their departmental goals.

Kotter listed three grave consequences from allowing silos to exist:

1. Silos destroy trust. The loyalty grows stronger to your department head and weaker to the senior leadership or the overall vision.
2. Silos cut off communication. People do great at communicating within their departments, but they do everything they can to work around other teams, only communicating as a last resort to accomplish their own objectives.
3. Silos foster complacency. Kotter said, "In an organization where people in different divisions have little contact with one another, it's easy to become inwardly focused and complacent with the status quo."[3]

I've seen this happen time and time again in churches. We develop "silo ministries." The youth ministry has its own purposes, goals, and plans that have absolutely nothing to do with the overall church. The women's ministry is a separate entity. The missions committee has its own projects that have nothing to do with the mission of the church. And everyone knows not to mess with the choir!

The church ends up with a "federation of sub-ministries."[4] They are all good ministries, but the strength of the whole is decreased because they lack a common vision and purpose. The church crawls along and makes incremental progress without really being able to have a turbocharged impact on the community.

I'm pretty sure this is not what our early church leaders had in mind in Philippians 2:2: "Then make me truly happy by agreeing wholeheartedly with each other, loving one another, and working together with one mind and purpose" (NLT).

It is no less detrimental in a business environment. A good friend recently shared with me about the silos that exist in his small construction business, which has fewer than fifteen employees, between his sales team and the guys in the field who have to install what's been sold. He relayed the frustration that he senses between the teams and the amount of time he spends trying to help the two teams communicate. Silos have to go, but first they must be identified.

How to Spot a Silo

Here is some evidence that silos exist in your organization:

IN A CHURCH
- Ministries are competing for the same dollars through fund-raising or pitching their ideas.
- Ministries are arguing over calendar space. Instead of deciding based on priorities, there is a competitive culture.
- Leaders are complaining for reasons such as, "My room got

messed up by the students," or "My supplies in the kitchen were used by the women's group."

IN A BUSINESS

- You deal with customers who are unhappy that what was promised wasn't delivered.
- The profitability of the company is going in the wrong direction, and good employees are beginning to leave.

IN BOTH CHURCHES AND BUSINESSES

- You begin to hear a lot of "us" and "them" language.
- Every department has its own mission statement, its own purpose, its own vision—without a very clear connection to the overall vision of the organization.
- You walk on eggshells around certain staff members or departments.
- Attitudes begin to go sour.
- You hear statements such as, "That's not my area," or "We didn't have anything to do with that decision."

———

This happens faster than you would think in a new church or start-up business. You think you are incredibly clear about your mission and vision and how this new venture is going to be a different experience from any they've ever known. You launch and begin growing, and you start adding people to your team. And these folks come with years of silo-laden experiences from businesses and families. People do what people know. And silos begin to rise.

The first step is identifying silos. The more difficult task is tearing them down, which is addressed in the next chapter.

THINK ABOUT IT

1. Do you currently have any silo departments that need to be addressed? What action will you take today?

2. Are all your key leaders tuned in to the danger of silos? What can you do to make sure they know how to identify a silo and understand why it is unhealthy?

CHAPTER FORTY

DESTROY SILOS

IT TOOK ME MONTHS TO IDENTIFY THE SILO IN ONE OF MY departments. I kept hearing comparison or fairness language, but it was typically third- or fourthhand, so I didn't give it much credit. I heard about a little bit of jealousy about another department's budget, and someone even suggested that the department must not be valued since their budget was lower.

But it wasn't until I assigned a leadership coach to jump deep into the department that I confirmed the depth and seriousness of the silo that had evolved. In an organization that was relatively healthy, this department had developed a toxic environment that became a breeding ground for comparison, gossip, backbiting, and a victim mentality. Something had to be done.

It is extremely important to have senior-level leaders who are tuned in to the danger of silos, and who work overtime to tear them down. Here are some tips on tearing down the silos:

Clearly identify the overall objective.

A few years ago at my church we developed a strategy called "Focus on Five." We chose the five things we were all going to focus on for the next season, and this gave every ministry a reason to work together with other departments to accomplish the goal. More recently, we did this through a five-year vision.[1] Patrick Lencioni warned that if you don't have a shared goal, everyone makes up his or her own.[2]

Consider office locations.

Sometimes the construction of silos is encouraged because of office location. If you have one team with offices in a completely separate building, isolating that team, it's likely you will be dealing with a silo department. Not too long ago I changed office locations for 60 percent of the church staff in order to tear down some silos that were beginning to form.

Replace a leader.

I believe the person running a department has the power to build or tear down a silo. Leaders above them can help with training or coaching. People around them can offer help and advice. But there is no one else who can speak up during a meeting that is turning negative. No one else can influence the team to work with other teams. No one else can lead the team to support the leaders or rally around the vision. There have been times when I was unable to coach a leader who had built a thick silo, and my only recourse was to replace him or her.

Communicate your foundational beliefs.

Communicate them everywhere and often. At Granger, every year we spent a month talking about the vision of our organization. Our mission statement was printed larger than life on a prominent wall. Our values were faux etched in the glass along a primary corridor. Every new person had a chance to attend a Discover Granger seminar where he or she heard about these core beliefs from our leader. Jack Welch said, "When you talk about your beliefs so often that you think you'll throw up the next time you say it—you're probably just about communicating at the right level."[3]

Even your most faithful volunteers or most tenured employees will forget why you exist if you don't constantly communicate it. It's not that they're rebellious; it's just too easy to fall back on what they've known or believed for years. Even the systems you use for scheduling space in the building, setting your annual budget, or requesting expense reimbursements can be great opportunities to restate values and priorities.

Hold weekly meetings with everyone.

I talked earlier in this book about the huge advantages of meeting with the entire team every week (see chapter 27). When your senior leaders can hear from every single person on the team, and they can hear each person's vision, it does wonders to keep silos from popping up.

———

Above all, make sure your core leaders truly believe they are serving one organization with one purpose. That will revolutionize how they interact with one another. The feeling will be, "We are all on the same team pulling the same direction."

THINK ABOUT IT

1. Do you have any silos that you've been reluctant to address? What action will you take today?

2. Have you ever been the creator of a silo because of a disagreement with the direction of the church or business? What communication needs to happen to get realigned, or to find another place that more closely matches your view?

CHAPTER FORTY-ONE

BE A GOOD FOLLOWER

I ONCE WORKED FOR AN ORGANIZATION THAT WAS AMAZING. But the department where I was assigned was a toxic environment that was certainly siloed in its focus and leadership. I was frustrated and wanted to quit. This wasn't what I signed up for.

A good friend talked me out of it. He encouraged me to wake up every day and focus on being faithful. I said, "It doesn't matter! No one will notice! These leaders are incapable of noticing anything but their own self-interests!"

He explained that my choices and my faithfulness should not be dependent on someone else's choices or leadership style. "Just keep doing the next right thing," he encouraged.

Many of the things I've shared about building a healthy culture are focused on what the leader or leaders can do. But not everyone is at the top of the organization.

"If you believe lack of authority prevents you from leading effectively, it is time to rethink your understanding of leadership,"[1] said Mike Bonem and Roger Patterson, authors of *Leading from the Second Chair.*

Most of us will work most of our lives for someone else. And sometimes we do this in very tough environments. The truth is everyone, at every level, can help build and sustain a healthy culture. Much of this has to do with modeling how to be a great follower.

What Is a Great Follower?

A MOMENTUM INCREASER

This has to do mostly with attitude. Don't make your leader be the only one pulling up the energy and attitude level of the rest of the team. Bring the energy. Everywhere you go, take your fun with you and help bump up the momentum.

A VALUES CHAMPION

No one should live out the values more than you do. Your business or church has decided certain values are important, and they have likely settled on a mission or vision. Be a champion of those values. Do everything you can to intentionally support the mission, and explain to others why you are doing this. Don't expect them to make the connection.

A SILO DESTROYER

Refer back to the previous chapter ("Destroy Silos") on this. As a contributing member of the team, it is important to do everything you can to sniff out and stomp out silos.

A STRAIGHT TALKER

Make a decision not to engage in triangle conversations. Don't talk to Joe about Bill's problems, hoping that Joe will tell Bill how disappointed you are. Be vigilant about not playing those middle school games. Just talk straight, tackle issues when they arise, and treat people like adults. When you have an issue with someone, go directly to that person, do not pass go, do not collect two hundred dollars, and for goodness' sake, do not drag other people into the cesspool of speculation. Make a decision not to participate in gossip, slander, or put-downs, even about someone you don't particularly like.

A GENEROUS GIVER

Jesus told us that where our money goes directly reflects the condition of our hearts (Luke 12:34). As a follower, if you choose to work for a church, you should do so at a place where you love the mission of that church, want to give generously to the ministry, and can't wait to see what's going to happen through the congregation.

AN INNOVATIVE THINKER

Great followers are solution oriented. They don't just take complaints and problems up the chain of command—they show up with solutions. I loved it when we were enduring budget cuts or staff transitions, and a staff member said, "No problem, we'll figure out a different way to do this." The most creative ideas are born through adversity. Some of the greatest ideas in ministry came when we didn't have enough staff or weren't able to buy all the stuff we needed. Leaders, who sometimes have to make extremely difficult decisions when times are lean, love followers who show up with innovative solutions.

A LOYAL FRIEND

I'm not saying you are best friends with your boss, or that you chest bump at the end of every football game, but your leader needs to know you are *for* him or her. So always assume the best, and when accusations are flying, believe in your team. Believe in your leader.

AN INTEGRITY KEEPER

You should be someone who still walks the walk when no one

else is looking. Your personal choices are bigger than you. They affect your kids and your family, and they can even have an impact on your job or the entire organization. Your leaders don't need you to be perfect, but they need you to live an authentic life of integrity. If you need to take some time off to work on something, ask for the time off before you make a choice that will cripple the entire organization.

AN UNBELIEVABLE SPOUSE AND/OR PARENT

The strength of your ministry and leadership comes from your strength at home. You do no one any good if you work all the time while your marriage is crumbling and your kids are a mess. Don't believe the lie that you can trade quantity time for quality time. Quality time never comes without quantity time. You have to spend scores of hours with your kids if you hope for occasional, spontaneous moments of heart-to-heart connection.

A LIFELONG LEARNER

Recall chapter 7 of this book, where we talked about the importance of self-education. Read books, listen to podcasts, call other leaders to pick their brains, and bring back the best stuff you can find. Be a constant source of ideas based on what you've learned from the best practices of other organizations. Go to conferences when you can, and come back with an unsolicited summary for your boss: "Here are the two or three things I learned last week."

If we have a team full of great followers who take these ideals to heart and make them authentic throughout their daily lives, we will have unstoppable unity and focus. And that might just revolutionize the workplace.

THINK ABOUT IT

1. Rank yourself A, B, or C on each of these characteristics of a great follower. If you gave yourself any Bs or Cs, what can you do to bump it up? (A=this describes me; B=doing okay; C=needs improvement)
2. If you are really brave, ask someone else to rank you. Have a discussion about the areas where you differ.

CHAPTER FORTY-TWO

SIGNS OF AN UNHEALTHY CULTURE

I HAD HEARD THREE DISTURBING REPORTS ALL IN THE same month. One guy resigned because he didn't agree with part of the vision. When we asked, "Why didn't you say anything?" he said he was afraid. Another report came from an employee who was feeling sexually harassed by her boss but didn't know who to tell. And the third report was about a leader who had been saying less-than-supportive things to her team about our senior team.

Alarm bells starting going off. Red lights flashed. We had a culture problem. If you had asked me in the previous month, I would have given our culture an A grade. But now, with three conversations, we were at best a C minus.

The whole third section of this book has been devoted to building a great culture, but you might still need help identifying whether your culture is healthy. Never stop evaluating; never stop paying attention.

Signs of an Unhealthy Culture

INSECURITY AND NERVOUSNESS

- Staff members are afraid they might lose their jobs if they entertain a potential offer from somewhere else. In a healthy culture, leaders come alongside their teams to help them think or pray through and consider the offers.

- Traveling to conferences or visiting other organizations is discouraged. Insecure leaders are threatened by the new perspectives that might reveal their own inadequacies.
- The only new ideas the leader likes are his or her own.
- In brainstorming sessions, people don't attend or are afraid to share. This could mean the leader is looking for affirmation about his or her own ideas rather than looking for new ones.
- Defensiveness is more of a norm than an exception. This points to people feeling as if they have to prove themselves.
- There is little freedom to try new things without fear of reprisal. In an unhealthy culture, you either (a) never try anything new or (b) say, "Let's try it and ask forgiveness later if it doesn't work." In a healthy culture, you initiate new ideas and propose new directions without fear because the typical response by leadership is to ask clarifying questions and then bless the effort.

EMPTY DESKS, QUIET HALLWAYS

- You have a revolving door of staff. A high turnover is a symptom of deeper troubles and wastes precious resources on downtime and continual retraining.
- You publish a notice regarding a new staff position, and hardly anyone expresses interest. The word is out: your business or church isn't a fun place to work.
- People clock out right at five o'clock, and you don't see your staff hanging out after hours or during their discretionary time.

- Very few former staff members talk positively about their experiences.
- There are lots of hushed hallway conversations.

LACK OF COMMUNICATION AND TRUST

- Your leaders and core staff can't quickly, easily, and authentically tell you the mission of the organization and why it matters. Likewise, if the vision lacks clarity, your culture needs work.
- You never (or rarely) meet together with your entire team.
- Everything has to go to the top for approval. Other leaders on the team have not been empowered to make decisions.
- Everyone knows of people on staff who lack competence or character, yet the leaders are unwilling to make the tough decisions to let them go.

DIRTY TRICKS

- There is a lot of backbiting, bickering, or complaining between team members.
- You get reports of harassment, discrimination, or leaders abusing their power or positions.
- There is an acceptance of pranks on the team that embarrass people or highlight their weaknesses.

UNHAPPY FAMILIES

- People have to choose between job and family. You probably don't say that out loud, but your team regularly is making that choice.
- Spouses of your staff feel as if they are competing with a mistress called "ministry" or "job."

- It is common for staff to attempt to negotiate better salaries or benefits. This often points to a lack of feeling valued.

———————

You don't get to spike the ball on culture. You can never proclaim your culture a success or stop working on it. If you have human beings working with and for you, then this will be something you work on ad infinitum.

If you do only one thing, assign a culture champion on your team. Whether it is yourself or someone else at the senior leadership level, someone should be thinking about assessing and improving the culture every step of the way.

THINK ABOUT IT

1. Take time with your team to honestly consider each of these characteristics. Evaluate your health.

2. Pick two things you can do as a team to improve your culture right away. It won't happen overnight, but with intentional steps, progress can happen.

PART FOUR

LEAD CONFIDENTLY THROUGH A CRISIS

WHEN I WAS SIXTEEN YEARS OLD, I WALKED INTO MY ROOM one day to find a little pamphlet on my bed. It was called "The Lonely Whine of the Top Dog" by Charles Swindoll. My mom had left it for me with a note inside. She could see the pressures I was facing as a leader in my youth group, the president of my class at school, and the manager of the basketball team. She wanted me to know that I wasn't alone, that she loved me, and that God had called me to leadership—and it wouldn't always be rosy.

The timing was right. That year one of my favorite teachers was killed in a car accident. Her death left a gaping hole in leadership at our church, and I was asked to step in and fill it. I didn't want to lead; I wanted to curl up in a ball in the corner and cry.

There is a common misconception that leadership is glamorous. Leaders get to be in the spotlight; they are on a pedestal in people's eyes; they make decisions for hundreds or thousands of people.

But anyone who has led for very long knows that is a crock. The sparkle fades quickly, and the shimmer is just a mirage. Leadership is difficult. And it is lonely.

In a recent five-year season, leadership for me included

- cutting the budget six times as income dropped more than 20 percent during the recession;
- laying off eight people who had families depending on their incomes;
- saying goodbye to a dear friend who could no longer lead, and watching him storm out of my office (I haven't seen him since);
- getting out of sync relationally with my boss;
- discovering a close associate was making unethical choices and having to dismiss him from staff;
- designing a building that we ultimately couldn't afford;
- finding out someone trusted was being careless with the church's money; and
- firing architects and designers who were good friends but couldn't control the budget.

Reading that list, it sounds like my job sucked, right? But it didn't. I loved what I was privileged to lead, but with any leadership role there are challenges.

And it is leading in tough times that creates the greatest leaders.

Case in point. Tell me what you know about Chester Arthur. Probably very few of you would even recall that he was the president of the United States from 1881 to 1885. He presided over the country in a fairly stable time in our history. Not much happened during those years. And so he is not memorable.

Many of history's leaders whom you do know are famous because they led through some of the most difficult times imaginable: Abraham Lincoln led our country through the Civil War; Winston Churchill led Europe out of World War II; Ronald Reagan brought an end to the Cold War; and George W. Bush and Rudy Giuliani stand out for their leadership after 9/11.

John Maxwell said that during tough times, "Leaders stretch to the challenge, while followers shrink from the challenge."[1]

If you are leading, you don't have a choice: you will face tough times. The question is whether you will be equipped to lead with strength. It's my prayer that the following chapters will give you practical tools to face the trouble ahead.

CHAPTER FORTY-THREE

LEADING CHANGE

I DON'T CARE WHAT ANYONE ELSE SAYS, CHANGE IS HARD. The reason people stay where they are is because they are comfortable. And except for a few maniacs who think the Ironman triathlon is fun, most people like staying comfortable.

We made many changes through the years at the church where I led, and I have some scars to show for them. We canceled services, changed locations, ended women's ministry (gasp!), discontinued a weekly gathering that had nine hundred people regularly attending, built buildings, released staff, and shifted the church toward a new vision.

As I've mentioned, I wrote a whole book on leading through one of the biggest changes we initiated,[1] but for this chapter let me share some general principles about leading through change.

Change is good.

Change may be hard for those ingrained in the institution, but change attracts new people. Go to any store and look at products, and you will see phrases such as "New and improved" and "33 percent more." You'll see the same product in a new packaging, with a new rebate, or partnered with a bonus product. Go to a restaurant or hotel and you'll see "Under new management." Go to a local business and you'll see they have moved products around the store, changed the signage, or upgraded the facade.

One of my friends who owns a restaurant franchise says he is required by the corporate office to spend a bunch of money and upgrade the building every seven years to infuse excitement with the regulars and attract the attention of new guests.

And it's true. Change:

- attracts attention;
- gets people talking about what you are doing;
- communicates that you aren't done growing;
- in a church, focuses people outwardly rather than inwardly; and
- generates and sustains momentum.

Do I suggest changing something just to change? Not very often, but sometimes, yes. Sometimes change is what will get people out of a rut and help them get to a new place so they can see things differently and think about things with a new perspective. Sometimes you can't change your worship services until you move them out of your sanctuary and into your gym. Sometimes you can't break a pattern of decline until you change up the team and infuse it with new leadership.

Why is a rut a rut? It is a rut because it's comfortable. It's the way people before you have traveled, not because they all coincidentally chose the same path, but because the people in front saw it as the most logical, most comfortable, and most efficient way to travel. And pretty soon you have a rut.

Change is messy.

To break out of a rut requires hard work and a bit of a mess. Sometimes you lose some people along the way because they liked the rut. I lost some of my dearest friends because of changes we made at the church along the way. Some of them I lost because of changes that I personally initiated—and it's really hard. It's messy.

Scott Wilson is a pastor in Texas who wrote a book called *Steering Through Chaos*. Regarding chaos, he wrote:

> If we think that everybody on our staff and in leadership in the church is going to stand up and cheer when we steer them through chaos, we're deluding ourselves. A few hardy souls may thrive on change. They love risks, and they can't wait to take the next one. The vast majority of people, however, are risk averse, especially when a transition may alter their role, which is a major part of their identity. Don't underestimate the threat of change to your people. It's not just moving names on an organizational chart. Change puts the two things they cherish most at risk: their reputation and their relationships.[2]

Change is risky.

You make your best guess, but in the end, you don't know if the change is right or not. I heard Steven Furtick say in a talk to leaders, "When God tells you to go a certain direction, you are never absolutely positive that you heard it right. On a good day, I might be 80 percent sure of the vision."[3] But you pray, seek God, and make the best decision you can, and then you begin to enact change. Sometimes you are wrong.

Change is a process.

I know this isn't rock solid and there are exceptions, but most of the time I have found that change works best when following these six steps:

1. Make the case for the change. You have to clearly describe why it is so important to change. What will be lost by staying where you are? What will be gained by making the change?
2. Create urgency for the change. You never want to bend the facts or skew the stats, but you do want to clearly show that you can wait no longer for the change.
3. Make the decision for the change. There comes a point when the time for waiting for additional buy-in is over, and the decision must be made.
4. Communicate the change. This is so crucial that I've devoted an entire chapter to this issue (see chapter 48).
5. Implement the change. Many leaders lose the battle here. They like casting vision for change and getting people excited, but they don't like the daily grind of implementation. Find someone who can carry the ball all the way to the end zone with methodical consistency.
6. Consider changing the change. After going through all the work of change, it's easy to convince yourself that the new way is sacred. It's not. And perhaps a few years down the road, it will be time to consider another change.

With big change, put all hands on deck.

You can't do a big change with one eye on the change and one eye on something else. Everyone needs to focus on it at the same time.

Jack Welch said, "Anytime you start something new, put your very best person on the job. Otherwise it will fail."[4] That's good advice for a large company. For a church, I would say something similar: anytime you change something major, put *all* your best people on the change.

THINK ABOUT IT

1. What area of your organization is stuck right now? What change could you instigate to get it moving?

2. Have you initiated change poorly? What did that look like, and how will you do it differently next time?

CHAPTER FORTY-FOUR

COUNT THE YES VOTES

UP UNTIL RECENTLY I HAD WORKED FOR NONPROFIT organizations my entire adult life—nearly thirty years. And there is one thing that is consistent: some people will join what you are doing, and others will not. Some will buy in, and others will ignore what you are doing.

That is really difficult for those who lead churches or ministries. They aren't there because they are trying to make a bunch of money but because it's a cause they believe in. And they are so passionate about it they think others should be involved also. So it's easy to focus on people who don't jump onboard.

But the fact is, you can't focus on the no votes. There are over 290 million people in America alone who haven't voted to participate in organizations I have worked with. That may seem obvious, but sometimes we get all bent out of shape because the no people seem so much louder than the yes people. And they will continue to get louder if you focus on them.

There are a number of reasons someone isn't going to attend a particular church. Geography is a big one. But it might also be because of size, personalities, preferences, methods, or a bunch of other reasons. And that's okay. A church's leaders should just want to say, "Here's where we are going. Do you want to come with us? Do you want to help us get there? Yes? Good, let's go."

At the church where I worked, we weren't counting the people who said no. We didn't have their names on a list. We weren't mad at them. We didn't think they were stupid. We didn't think they were lesser as Christians. They just wanted to go somewhere else, and that was fine. We were looking for the yes votes.

Does that mean that we didn't want feedback? Absolutely not. I used to have conversations every week with yes people about what they wished was different about the church. We changed things every day. I imagine there weren't many organizations that were quicker at changing things that weren't working or weren't effective. I believe there is a kernel of truth in just about every interaction I have with people. So I look for that. Sometimes something a person tells you has a high percentage of truth, and other times you have to look hard to get past the individual's filters and biases.

I first heard talk about looking for the "kernel of truth" from Nancy Leigh DeMoss.[1] She is a high-profile leader, and anyone who is getting something significant done is going to get criticized. She taught me to listen, pray, and see if there is a kernel of truth in the midst of the accusation, even if most of it is ridiculous. If that truth is there, learn from it and move on.

That is an important practice. Too often leaders get sidetracked by the no people. We cater to their whining, we spend all our energy trying to keep them happy, and we do damage control because of the side conversations they are having. Don't misunderstand; I think it's important to listen. Sometimes (perhaps often) God will speak through someone when we least expect it. But there is a crossover point after we've listened, considered, and prayed. We know what God has called our church or business to do and be, and we must pursue that with confidence.

Some will go with us. And some won't. And we'll sometimes experience deep pain when the person who chooses to leave is our closest friend or relative—the person we never imagined moving on without.

Just put one foot in front of the other. Learn from the kernel of truth, count yes votes, and keep moving.

THINK ABOUT IT

1. In some of the criticism you've recently received, is there a kernel of truth you should be paying attention to?

2. Do you get easily sidetracked by the no votes? Can you pull some people around you to help you shoulder the criticism?

CHAPTER FORTY-FIVE

RESIGNATIONS AND CHARACTER ISSUES

IT IS RARELY GOOD NEWS WHEN YOU LOSE A STAFF MEMBER (although I can think of a few notable exceptions). Most of the time, even if the decision is good for the organization, there is pain and emotion involved.

I've probably been involved in more than a hundred and fifty termination or resignation conversations, and as I reflect back, most of them would fall into one of these four categories:

1. They resigned.
2. They were fired for lapses in character or moral judgment.
3. They were fired for attitude or loyalty issues.
4. They were fired for competence or capacity limitations.

Let's take a look at the first two.

Resignation

It is never easy when someone resigns. There is an initial emotional response of rejection when someone no longer wants to play on your team. It is natural to want to isolate the individual, huddle up with the remaining players, and make excuses for why he or she is choosing to leave. And yet sometimes it is God who puts in someone a "holy discontent"—and it stirs that person to move on to do something else.[1]

I strongly encourage you to refuse to wallow in the gutter of self-pity and blame. Take the high road, celebrate the person's years of service, and send him or her off with a party. Demonizing someone who is no longer on the team does nothing to build the body of Christ and does little to create unity going forward.

I enjoy strong relationships today with former leaders who left my team over the years. Mike Adkins was a pastor at Granger for years, and he is now the lead pastor for Grace Church in Orlando, with more than a thousand people worshiping each weekend in four locations. Jeff Bell joined our team to launch our first multisite campus in 2008. Now he is a key leader at Northland Church in Orlando, helping lead their multisite efforts. Tony Morgan, the chief strategic officer of The Unstuck Group, was Granger's pastor of administrative services before leaving in 2006. He now consults with churches all across the country to help them take steps in strategy and structure. And Butch Whitmire left my team in 2009 after believing he had done all he could as Granger's pastor of creative arts. He reentered the business community and is now the chairman of Granger's board.

When someone resigned, I encouraged a short disengagement. In *Simply Strategic Stuff*, I wrote a chapter called "Make 'Hellos' Long and 'Goodbyes' Quick."[2] I gave two reasons why it is important to schedule the final workday within two weeks of a person's resignation:

1. People who are departing become a magnet for every unhappy person in your organization. Whether they are leaving

on good or bad terms, those who have complaints will assume they are leaving for the complainers' own reasons. So they will begin to unload on departing staff members. They will look for a comrade to side with. They will gossip with others, pretending they have "inside information" from the former staff member.

2. A staff member who is leaving for another organization can no longer dream about the future of your organization. They become dead weight within hours of the announcement. There will be no additional conversations about new ways to reach more people for Christ or creative ways to do the Christmas series. In business, they will no longer be thinking about improving customer relations or solving problems. No, their dreams are, understandably, somewhere else.[3]

Character Issues

When someone messes up and exemplifies a lack of character, it often means you can no longer employ them. Over the many years I've been in church leadership, we've had to let people go for extramarital relationships, sexual harassment, embezzlement, and other activities representing a lack of personal boundaries.

These issues always come as a surprise, but when the evidence is undeniable, action must be taken. I pray you never face this, but if you do, here are some things I've learned:

DO NOT WAIT TO GO PUBLIC.

Once you know, you must go public. Otherwise, if the information leaks out first, it looks like a cover-up. You can say all day that you "had planned to tell the congregation next week," but no one will believe you, and you will have lost credibility. If an employee has stolen money from your business, it's possible he or she has also stolen from your customers. You will need a communication plan.

The individual's sphere of influence dictates how broadly you will communicate. When it was a worship leader who messed up, we told the whole church. When it was a high school director, we told the students and their parents.

CONSIDER THE PERSON'S FAMILY.

Even though the person messed up and damaged the reputation of your organization, consider his or her family when determining severance and extension of health insurance or other benefits. It's tempting to cut the person off and be done. Whether you lead a church or a business, consider caring for the family and showing unexpected love.

CONSIDER THE VICTIMS.

If there was an extramarital affair involved, the spouse is the victim. She (or he) did nothing wrong, yet in a nanosecond lost her marriage, her friends, and possibly her church. She will walk around town thinking everybody is talking about her. Go the extra mile to offer her help, counseling, friendship, financial support, or whatever you can to minister to her needs.

If a minor was involved, or you believe it's possible a minor was involved, you should report this immediately to your local prosecutor or child protective services office. In most states this is a requirement, and you can jeopardize the assets and reputation of your organization by not following through.

THINK ABOUT LEGAL ISSUES.

Seek legal advice so you don't put your church or business at risk by anything you say or do.

Use a termination agreement with the individual. The person's severance should be dependent on agreeing to take the high road in his or her speech and behavior.

———————

I have found that most people in the church are not shocked or disillusioned that the church is having problems. They just don't want the leaders to try to hide it. And in business, your customers and staff members will respect you more if you take the high road of integrity when dealing with a wayward employee.

THINK ABOUT IT

1. Is your company gracious when someone resigns? Do you focus on the person's years of service or on the hurt that he or she is leaving?

2. Have you ever waited too long to let someone go for a lapse in character? What were the results?

CHAPTER FORTY-SIX

BAD ATTITUDES AND LIMITED CAPACITY

AS I INTRODUCED IN THE PREVIOUS CHAPTER, MOST termination conversations fall into one of these four categories:

1. They resigned.
2. They were fired for lapses in character or moral judgment.
3. They were fired for attitude or loyalty issues.
4. They were fired for competence or capacity limitations.

We've already considered resignations and lapses in character. Let's study the last two.

Attitude or Loyalty

I heard my boss say dozens of times, "I can get someone to gripe and complain and have a bad attitude for free. I don't need to pay someone for that." And it is so true. Sometimes churches have what Bill Hybels calls a case of "terminal niceness."[1] We want to be nice and gracious and give people an opportunity to improve. But if you are giving people a paycheck, or you have put them in positions of significant leadership as volunteers, and they are pulling people down around them through negativity or biting sarcasm, you have the right to free those people from their jobs.

I had an employee who was amazing most of the time. But every few weeks he would come in with an attitude that made Grumpy the dwarf look like an incurable optimist. I would hear reports of how he treated other staff members, or how he talked about me to others, and it became a problem. Each time I talked to him about it things got better for a while, but eventually I had to let him go. It saddened me because he was a good friend and had such great potential.

Sometimes you will be the last person to know that the individual working for you has a bad attitude. Be sure to listen to your team; they will often alert you to issues you didn't even know existed.

And sometimes it is you who has the bad attitude. If you think you might, you probably do. There is never a good reason to talk negatively about your boss, your job, or other team members. Your job is to be *for* your boss, to support her, and to help her do her job better. If you need to vent, tell your spouse when you get home or call an out-of-state friend. But while you are on the clock, getting paid by your boss, you are being paid to have a great attitude.

Competence or Capacity

This is, by far, the most difficult to manage. Employees may have a great attitude, tremendous character, love for you, and loyalty to the business. They just can't do the job to your satisfaction. And that is so subjective. Other people may think they are doing great, but as their supervisor, you believe they don't have the skills or abilities to take the ministry or business to the next level.

Sometimes the fault is your own. You elevated them to positions they weren't gifted for or into roles they weren't ready for.

And the positions they've left are now filled, so there is no alternative but to let them go.

This is where you might make an exception to the short-goodbyes rule. If the person has a great attitude and demeanor, you might give him or her time to find other employment before you announce he or she is leaving. For example, in September you might have the conversation letting an employee know he is no longer a good fit for the role. But as long as he keeps contributing with strength and positivity, you will let him look for other employment until the end of December. At that point, you'll need to release him even if he hasn't found something else.

If he does find other employment, then you can agree with him to communicate that he is resigning to go do something else. No one needs to know that you initiated the termination.

Be exceptionally gracious to these individuals. They have done what they were asked and supported the church well, so do everything you can to help them exit with dignity and care.

It is never easy to let someone go. I typically experience a couple sleepless nights before I have a conversation with someone. When you make a decision that you know is going to cause someone else great pain, it is very difficult. And it's even harder when you know his kids might go to bed crying because Daddy lost his job.

Just remember: your organization does not exist to employ people. As a pastor or leader, you do not owe anyone a job. It is not your burden to make sure someone makes a decent amount of money to provide for his or her family. Of course you love and care for people, but your first responsibility is to further the mission of the church. It is to help people meet Jesus and take steps in their faith. As a business leader, your job is to fulfill the vision of the company, perhaps create value for shareholders, or provide a service for your customers. You gather people (staff and volunteers) around you to help further the cause, but if they are no longer contributing, you must release them.

THINK ABOUT IT

1. Have you been avoiding a difficult conversation with someone on your staff?

2. Is there someone on your team with a stinky attitude? What will you do to make sure that person's attitude no longer impacts the rest of the team?

CHAPTER FORTY-SEVEN

UNAVOIDABLE LAYOFFS

PAIN. THAT IS THE ONLY WORD TO DESCRIBE THE WEEKS AT the end of January 2009. We met, prayed, agonized, prayed some more, and pled with God to help us find some other way. But in the end, we had to tell eight friends their positions had been eliminated. We could no longer pay them to do their jobs. And fifteen others were told on the same day of reductions in their hours.

The global economic crisis was wreaking havoc in our small Midwest community. The *New York Times* described our area as "the white-hot center of the meltdown of the American economy."[1] Every day we would hear of someone else in our church losing his or her job. Trickle-down economics was working on us in reverse: a poor economy slammed businesses; loss of jobs meant lower incomes; loss of income meant lower offerings; and lower tithes and offerings meant we couldn't pay as many staff.

The decision was not immediate or rushed. It was the end result of a slide in contributions that began about eighteen months earlier. We did everything we could to avoid this move—cutting budgets, freezing salaries, eliminating capital expenses, and delaying projects. But in the end, it wasn't enough.

Those few weeks were the most stressful and difficult I had faced up to that point. Even though our senior team was unified on the decision, and it didn't all rest on my shoulders, I still felt very alone. We all did. I remember walking to my car at the end of the day after the final layoff decisions were communicated, wondering if someone with raging emotions would be waiting for me in the parking lot.

There are several things we learned during those difficult days:

THE EMOTIONAL FALLOUT

- Our employment advisor said on that day, "You can provide an environment for healing, but you can't be the healers." That was hard to hear, but she was right. In this case, the one who caused the pain couldn't also be the one to heal the pain.

- Laying off people is messy. There is no easy way to tell people they no longer have a job. I hated those conversations. I regret that, in these layoffs, I lost the friendship of someone who meant a great deal to me. I have no idea how it could have been avoided, but it saddens me greatly.

- When you let people go who are pulling their weight, and you don't replace them, that means your remaining staff and volunteers are picking up the slack. You have to realize performance and productivity are going to suffer. You can't just keep moving on as though nothing happened.

- We were advised to have our senior pastor remain clear of the termination conversations. The reason we were given for this: he needed to be their pastor after this was done, not the guy who fired them. My one regret is that we listened to this advice. One woman we let go was a charter member. I think if her pastor had visited her and her husband, loved them, and had the tough conversation, there is a chance they may not have been so deeply hurt.

THE REACTION FROM OUTSIDE

- People from afar suggested, "I'm sure it was hard, but you probably got rid of some dead weight." Uh, no. We didn't get rid of any dead weight. The time to get rid of dead weight is when you notice it's dead; you don't wait for layoffs. The people we lost were great people who were contributing significantly to the mission.

DOING RIGHT BY THOSE LEAVING

- It was right and honorable that the church covered full pay and insurance for the displaced employees for months following their departures. It was difficult financially, but I don't regret it a bit.
- Everyone was also given the option to team up with an employment agency in town to get help with résumé development, landing interviews, and even dealing with the natural emotions attached to being laid off.

THE SILVER LINING

- I believe the transition for a few individuals took the lid off their capacity and potential. For example, one individual joined the staff of a church in Florida and excelled in video production and direction far beyond what he did with us. I had to lay off my good friend and administrative assistant, but he became the creative director for a large church and helped them make tremendous strides in their weekend services.
- Tough times surface creative solutions. Because we let

our receptionist go, we had to figure out a way to fill the role with staff and volunteers. It took awhile, but we soon developed a team of amazing volunteers to handle that function. Although finances improved, five years later we still had not replaced the position.

If You're Facing a Layoff

Leadership is a high calling. One of our jobs is to make sure the organization doesn't get into financial crisis. I hope you never have to go through the pain of layoffs. I pray I never have to again. But sometimes the responsibility of stewardship requires such a decision.

BE QUICK.

You don't want to drag out this process. Your morale will be in the tank from the time you say, "Layoffs are coming" until you make final determinations. We announced the process to the entire staff on a Wednesday, took a few days to confer with supervisors, and then delivered the news on Monday morning. It was five days.

CARE WELL.

If you wait too long to make this decision, you won't have the flexibility to offer a generous severance. Our practice at Granger was always to err on the side of grace. We would rather have been too gracious in any termination than overly just.

COMMUNICATE CLEARLY.

Be clear about why layoffs are required, how the decision will be made, who will find out first, and what will happen after. Be sure to communicate well with your board, congregation, or core clients if needed.

GIVE TIME.

Your remaining staff will need help recovering. They spent a few days fearing for their own jobs and probably lost a few friends as a result of the layoffs. Don't underestimate the level of emotions that will be felt. Give people time to work through their grief.

THINK ABOUT IT

1. Do you have someone watching your contributions and expenses closely? How can he or she act to help avoid a layoff?

2. Would you be able to tell twelve to eighteen months before a financial crisis was on top of you? How can you make a plan for this?

CHAPTER FORTY-EIGHT

COMMUNICATION IS KEY

I'VE LONG BELIEVED THAT MORE LEADERS MESS UP because of bad communication than because of bad decisions. Very few leaders fail because they made the wrong decisions. But many fail because they didn't take the time to communicate their decisions to the right people, at the right time, in the right order. In my experience, I'd say 20 percent of leadership is making the right decisions. The other 80 percent is appropriately communicating those decisions.

In the previous chapter, I spoke of our decision to eliminate eight positions during a difficult time. For a significant change like this, appropriate communication is needed. We had people who walked into work on a Monday morning with a job and left minutes later unemployed. We had remaining staff members who just learned they would no longer be working with their best friends. We had family members who were hurting for their dad or mom or spouse. We had eight people we loved and cherished now entering a job climate that was harsh—where one in six people were unemployed and looking for work. We had volunteers who were rightfully in pain for their friends.

Great communication is needed for challenging leadership

transitions, but it is also needed for good changes like adding services, buying land, or constructing a new building. You can make a lousy decision but do well with communication and implementation, and it can be a success. On the other hand, you can make a great decision and lose the battle because your communication is weak.

Communication isn't an exact science. It requires strategy, assessment, execution, reassessment, more execution, and finally evaluation of what worked and what didn't.

Strategies for Great Communication

Here are two very important steps in rolling out change in your organization:

1. DON'T FORGET THE MEETING BEFORE THE MEETING.

I learned this about twenty years ago from John Maxwell while sitting in a conference in Anderson, Indiana. With any change, there are people you need to convince. Chances are, you instinctively know who those influencers are; the change is going to go well if those people are onboard, and it's going to go poorly if they aren't onboard.

Such a person may not be the positional leader. She may not have authority over anything or anyone. But she is a major influencer. Perhaps this is because of how long your influencer has been in the organization, or the strength of her personality, or who she is related to. For whatever reason, that person influences many other people, and you need to meet with her before you meet with everyone else. It's the meeting before the meeting.

This one principle will help you so much. It is timeless. You never have enough tenure for this not to be true. Anytime you want to start something new, make a change, add a program, or expand the budget, make sure you don't skip the meeting before the meeting. Be sure to meet with every key influencer ahead of time. Ask them all what they think, tell them you need their insights, ask them what questions they have and what additional information they need. Not only will you rally each of them to your cause, you will learn valuable information about how to communicate with the rest of the group.

2. PAY CLOSE ATTENTION TO SEQUENCING YOUR COMMUNICATION.

With any big change, you need a plan for communication. Who should you tell first? Who should you tell next? Who would be hurt if they found out about it from someone else besides you?

Think about this in your own family. Let's pretend you are the dad and you find out you just got transferred. You are going to move your family of six from Minneapolis to Philadelphia. You would think very carefully about sequencing this communication. You wouldn't tell your kids before you tell your wife. You wouldn't tell your third grader before you tell your teens. You wouldn't tell your neighbors or friends at church before you tell all your kids. No, you would carefully sequence the communication, giving each person time to emotionally respond. You would then recruit his or her help in telling the next person.

With any big decision at our church, we would typically sequence the communication like this:

1. Senior leadership team
2. Board members
3. Entire staff
4. Key leaders, influencers, and stakeholders (We would take the time to write their names out and determine who is going to talk with them.)

5. Other invested volunteers
6. Entire congregation (in a business, your client base)

I don't think anyone ever gets to keep the Great Communicator trophy. It's something you might get for a season, but you start from ground zero the next time a big change is imminent.

Key Concepts for Communicating Change

Once you've had the meeting before the meeting and you've sequenced your communication, make sure to pay attention to these simple communication principles:

- Start with a written communication strategy.
- Don't delay your communication. Waiting says you are hiding something.
- Be straight with people. No one will be surprised you are facing troubles. They are just watching to see how you will handle them.
- Ask people to help you. Everyone has potential to fuel the fire of gossip and bitterness or to put it out. Call your leaders to be firefighters for a short time, and provide them water (or information) so they can be effective.
- Plan time for conversations to help people process. You've been living in the pain for a while and are ready to move on. But they are experiencing it for the first time. Give them space to vent.

If you aren't going through a tough transition right now, I can promise you that one is just around the corner. Spend time making the best decisions you possibly can with the information you have available. But then spend most your time focusing on communication. That is where the battle is won or lost.[1]

THINK ABOUT IT

1. Has there been a change you tried to implement when you didn't have the meeting before the meeting? What were the consequences?

2. Have you been on the other end of a change when the communication was lousy? How did it make you feel about the change?

CHAPTER FORTY-NINE

GO OFF-LINE

YOU ARE HAVING CONFLICT WITH SOMEONE. IT'S A TENSE relationship. You dread talking to that person. You avoid seeing him. It may not be too bad right now, but occasionally it heats up. Maybe it's someone in your church. Maybe a staff member. Maybe a customer.

I'm right, aren't I? We all have those types of working relationships.

And many times, because we don't like to face these people or talk to them, we resort to e-mail communication. And that just makes the relationship worse.

I wrote in *Simply Strategic Stuff* that you should never e-mail when you are in any type of relational conflict with the individual. What is the alternative? "Talk with him or her in person so that you can see the eyes, watch the body language, and sense the person's spirit."[1]

Tim Sanders wrote in a blog post, "Over email, I have no earthly idea what you intend. This is especially true in the pithy thumbwritten world of BlackBerry. It wouldn't be surprising that you and I can get crossways in the up and down world of business. Stuff happens. If we are 100% over email, bad stuff happens to relationships when day-to-day stuff happens."[2]

He advised to take all communication with that individual off-line for one week. Use the phone or have face-to-face meetings, use no e-mail or texting for one entire week, and see if the relationship improves.

It's pretty good advice.

There is also some good advice found in Proverbs: "A gentle answer turns away wrath, but a harsh word stirs up anger" (15:1).

Nearly every week I have meetings, conversations, or e-mail exchanges where this verse is at the forefront of my mind. They are the types of interactions that could end in a very bad place. Emotions are high, the tension is thick, and many times I'm aware that the outcome rests squarely on my shoulders and my choices.

I've seen so many situations where a conversation gets out of control and hurtful words are said in a moment of anger, all because a leader didn't know how to defuse the situation with a gentle answer—or because the leader chose not to. I wonder how many staff members have been fired and friendships completely severed because neither individual knew how to minimize the damage through carefully chosen words. I meet people all the time who won't even speak to a former employer because of the pain.

If we were able to reverse time and observe the conversations that preceded a broken relationship, I wonder how many times we would find that this one Bible verse was ignored.

Giving a Gentle Answer

When I'm in these situations, I try to remind myself of these points:

- I don't have to say everything that comes into my head.
- I don't have to have the last word.
- It actually helps if I seek first to understand rather than to be understood.[3]

- E-mail is a bad tool for resolving conflict. It almost always escalates the tension.
- Phrases such as "you always" and "you never" are rarely helpful.
- Questions are almost always better than statements.
- I really don't know it all.
- The issue is probably not the issue. If I listen, I might learn the real issue.
- It doesn't matter how obvious it seems to me; I do not know the other person's motives.

THINK ABOUT IT

1. Can you think of a time when you've personally seen a "gentle answer turns away wrath" and keep a conversation from going nuclear? What can you learn from that?

2. Make a commitment to never handle another tense conversation by e-mail, and ask someone to help you keep your commitment.

CHAPTER FIFTY

THE PAIN OF GROWTH

A PASTOR ASKED ME TO TALK TO HIS STAFF AND ANSWER this question: "If our church is going to double in the next two years [from five hundred to a thousand], what will it take?" The same question might be asked from a business leader: "If we want to double sales in the next two years, what will it take?" This is what I shared:

1. Some of you won't have as much access to the senior leader. This has to be okay with you.

   Are you more committed to maintaining the tight-knit staff size and your proximity to the pastor or CEO? Or are you more committed to the organization growing?

2. Some of you are doing okay as leaders in your organization today, but it's possible that what you are currently doing won't cut it when you have doubled in size. You need to be willing to step into another role.

   Are you more committed to keeping your position and title? Or are you more committed to the growth of your business or church?

3. You will need to anticipate the strain and pressure that is coming before anyone actually feels it. As the leaders, you need to be looking ahead, seeing what is around the next corner.

   Are you comfortable? If so, you probably aren't anticipating growth adequately.

4. You will have to be as willing to stop stuff as you are to start stuff.

   What are you doing that takes time and energy and diverts your focus? What has God uniquely gifted your team to do where you should put more focus?

5. You will have to drive up the level of excellence. When people walk up to a fair booth to buy food, they have one expectation of service and quality. At McDonald's, it's another level. And when they walk into Ruth's Chris Steak House, it's yet another level. As you grow, so will the expectations of your guests.

   What are you doing right now that would not be considered excellent if you were an entity twice your current size?

6. You have to spend money on infrastructures like computers, data-management software, and staff to develop and run systems.

   What systems do you have right now that aren't broken yet but are showing signs of strain?

I liked the question this leader was asking. He was basically saying, "How do we prepare for growth?" Someone told me years ago, "If you want to grow, you always need to act like you are twice the size you currently are." It was good advice.

The Dangers of Growth

But growth is a two-sided coin. Many times, when we are growing, we get lazy. When things are going really well in the organization, we can put it on cruise control. When that happens:

- We don't pay attention to mission drift that is happening in individuals or even entire departments.
- We don't heed warning signs that are all too obvious later when looking in the rearview mirror.
- We don't ask enough questions.
- We rush spending and hiring decisions.
- We delay necessary firing decisions.
- We feel invincible. So we reject all criticism, even if we know there is a kernel of truth included.
- We often neglect important relationships. Since velocity and intimacy are enemies, many times a fast-growing organization can result in broken relationships.
- We stop being innovative. Why? Because we don't need to innovate. Growth is happening without it.

In an article in *Fast Company* magazine, Dan Heath and Chip Heath put it this way: "When you're getting rich, it's pretty easy to soothe the ol' gut. If you need a rationalization, your mind will provide one."[1]

For a church, you may not be getting rich, but your numbers might be trending upward. Attendance is increasing year after year, offerings are going up, and momentum is on your side.

I've been there. For the first twenty years at Granger, we averaged 23 percent growth year after year. Hindsight is a wonderful thing, and now I can see clearly how I sometimes fell into these traps.

The Traps of Decline

On the other hand, when your church has stopped growing or is in decline, there are also some traps that are easy to fall into:

- We forget the mission. We are frustrated by the lack of growth and so we allow the mission to be lost in charts, budgets, and forecasts.
- We mess with too many variables. We change eight things all at once. Perhaps two of them were great ideas and six were bad ideas. The end result might be neutral, and we will have no idea what worked and what didn't.
- We pay too much attention to the loudest voices. We never listened to the complainers before, but suddenly we wonder if they might be right.
- We candy coat the issues. In an effort to be positive and paint the picture of a brighter future, we make things appear rosier than they are.
- We focus more on the back door (*Why are they leaving?*) than the front door (*Why aren't they coming?*).
- We become too internally focused. We spend more and more time pleasing existing customers and much less time working on winning new customers.
- We turn down innovative ideas because we are too focused on maintenance and have lost our will to risk.
- We spend time trying to pin blame on the lack of growth rather than getting to the source of the problem.
- We look everywhere else for the issue and don't take time to look inside. *What if it's me?* is too hard to ask.
- We lose faith. We reflect on yesterday as though it could never happen again.

Accepting Risk

A few years ago the senior team at Granger spent hours considering: Have we become risk averse? Are we too afraid to make sweeping changes, if necessary, to catapult us into the future? Are we more concerned about our exposure and the number of organizations watching us than we are about figuring out our next step? Do we ask "What does God want?" before or after we ask "How much will it cost?" or "How many people will we lose?"

Our answers that day were as resounding in unity as in confidence.

- We will not be the team that is afraid of risk.
- We will not be the team that doesn't listen to the voice of God because we are too tuned in to the whining of people.
- We will not be the team that leads an organization so big and flabby that it is impossible to move.
- We will not be the team that misses an opportunity because we are in an endless cycle of risk-management assessment.
- We will not be the team that keeps waiting for the right time to lead the church to the next challenge.

It is important to consider what you really believe about growth. Is your team committed to the pain that comes from getting your church or business to the next level?

THINK ABOUT IT

1. Read through the lists and the questions in this chapter and do a gut check with your team.

2. Are you risk averse to the point that you might be missing God? How or how not?

CHAPTER FIFTY-ONE

WORK ON ALIGNMENT

THIS IS A TOPIC I'VE WRITTEN ABOUT PREVIOUSLY, BUT IT is so important that it would be a mistake not to include it in a book about leadership.[1] I have seen misaligned leaders mess up organizations or cause church splits probably faster than just about anything else.

I live in northern Indiana, and because of our proximity to Lake Michigan, we have hard winters. The roads freeze and thaw and freeze again many times over through the winter months of November through March. When that happens, the water seeps into the cracks, freezes, and expands, and the road explodes with a pothole. Along comes your car, and before you know it, you've hit the pothole at a high speed. Thanks to weather and the laws of physics, your tires are now out of alignment.

You may not even know at first. But before long you find you're constantly fighting to keep the car on the road. It wears you out and causes tension in your neck and shoulders as your hands keep a constant pressure on the steering wheel. And, all the while, your car is being damaged.

That's exactly what happens when you have an individual in your organization who is out of alignment with the direction of the leadership.

Three Types of Alignment

1. SAME DIRECTION

The best of situations is when everyone is heading in the same direction. There is peace and harmony. The organization (big arrow) is clear in its direction. There has probably been a mission developed and values agreed upon. There might even be a vision statement that is guiding the direction of the business or church. When everyone is aligned, all the leaders and core volunteers or employees (small arrows) are heading in the same direction. In business, conversations center on how to be more effective and beat the competition. Churches spend more time talking about how to reach more people rather than about the specifics of the church constitution or people's likes and dislikes of methods.

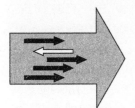

2. POLAR OPPOSITE

Sometimes, though, someone is going in the exact opposite direction of the organization and the other employees or volunteers. It is obvious to everyone. It's not a major deal, though, because the individual is so far off that no one is being influenced. You probably will need to have a tough conversation with the individual, but it won't be hard to convince him that he is not headed in the same direction. And no one else on the team will question your decision.

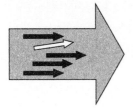

3. JUST A LITTLE OFF

There is a type of misalignment that is very dangerous. If unaddressed, it can destroy the unity of a church or a business, and sometimes split it apart.

This misaligned individual is just slightly off. She isn't advocating doctrines that are diametrically opposed to the church's statement of faith. She doesn't want to take the business in an entirely different direction. She just wants the leadership to move a few degrees. You've listened, asked clarifying questions, and heard her concerns. Even though you have restated the mission and vision, she continues to question methods, principles, values, staff motives, and decisions.

Normally she isn't even necessarily making an accusation. She's just asking questions in a way that tells you what she thinks without leaving herself defenseless if she is cornered. And, of course, every time she has a concern, she makes it clear she is representing unnamed others who agree with her: "You'd be shocked if you knew how many people agree with me!" she exclaims.

The misaligned individual never seems happy or satisfied. And you've never done quite enough to please her. This is the person you want to shake and say, "Can't you see all the great stuff that is happening?" But she can't see it.

Many years ago a volunteer visited my office and saw these alignment arrows on my computer. He pointed to the slightly askew arrow and said, "That's me!" He was right. He had a pet issue that we were never doing enough to address, and he eventually left the church in frustration.

Four Quadrants of Alignment

In a conference, I heard Jack Welch talk about misaligned individuals in different terms.[2] He drew the following chart on the wall and said there are four types of employees.

The Performance-Values Matrix

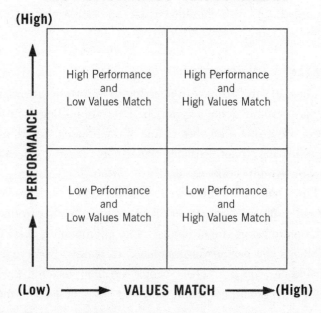

(High)

PERFORMANCE

High Performance and Low Values Match	High Performance and High Values Match
Low Performance and Low Values Match	Low Performance and High Values Match

(Low) ⟶ **VALUES MATCH** ⟶ **(High)**

QUADRANT 1 (UPPER RIGHT)

These individuals are performing at a high level. They are very competent, have great attitudes, and live out the values of the organization. They should be rewarded.

QUADRANT 2 (LOWER RIGHT)

These people aren't performing very well in their roles, but they love the company and have great attitudes. These are people who should be transferred to another role or retrained.

QUADRANT 3 (LOWER LEFT)

These people should have been fired yesterday. They contribute very little in their performances, and they either have stinky attitudes or don't get the direction of the company. They are badly misaligned, and you shouldn't delay on letting them go. They should be fired.

QUADRANT 4 (UPPER LEFT)

These are the people I'm referring to in my alignment arrows. They are actually doing a good job. They are pulling their weight and contributing to the bottom line of the organization. However, they either have poor attitudes or don't live out the values of the company. And it is noticeable.

This Quadrant-4 individual is the person you need to keep on your radar screen. This person may need your loving care and confrontation to bring him or her back into alignment. If these efforts fail, this is the person you may need to remove from your team as quickly as you can. These people are like poison and will fill a team with doubt, cynicism, fear, and low morale. You may not even notice how far down he or she has dragged the team until this person is removed and joy returns.

Misalignment rarely goes away. You will need to address it head-on. Yes, do it with grace, asking questions and seeking to understand. But once the talking is done, ask for support or encourage him or her to find another place to serve or work.

THINK ABOUT IT

1. Is there a leader in your organization who came to mind as you read this chapter? What will you do to address his or her misalignment?

2. Sometimes misalignment is God's prompting to move on and start something. Are you the crooked arrow? Is God prompting you to move someplace new?

CHAPTER FIFTY-TWO

THE FIVE STAGES OF FAILURE

PERHAPS YOU'VE HEARD OF THE FIVE STAGES OF GRIEF: denial, anger, bargaining, depression, and acceptance. I wonder if a similar list could help define the stages a leader goes through when his or her organization is failing. I know such a list has helped me when reflecting on tough times.

During the middle of a particularly difficult season at Granger, we spent time trying to get our minds and hearts around some unmet expectations. It may not have been outright failure, but it sure felt like it. What do you do when not as many people are inviting their friends, not as many have a biblical worldview, not as many are tithing, not as many are reading their Bibles, not as many are attending, and not as many are being baptized? If you run a company, what do you do when you aren't meeting expectations or sales are decreasing?

These questions are very real when you are going through a tough season, and the following list represents some of the stages of failure I have personally experienced:

Justified Reasoning

Well, our numbers are down because of the weather. People aren't reading their Bibles because we have so many seekers. The economy is in the tank so people aren't buying (or giving).

Sometimes there are rational reasons for failure, but if you continue to explain it away, over time it begins to look like an excuse rather than a reason. You can justify a week or even an entire season, but it's difficult to justify trends that are happening over a longer period of time.

Questioning

Perhaps the stats are wrong. Maybe we didn't ask the question in the right way. I bet a certain category of people refused to take the survey, and so the results are skewed.

When we don't like the data, it is so easy to question its validity. We look deep for one anomaly. We find the one place where we can cast doubt on the data, thus casting a large shadow over all the findings. Then it's easier to say everything is okay: "The problem isn't the organization, it's the data."

Blaming

It's the fault of the congregation. They stopped giving. They stopped inviting their friends. They think they're mature and deep, but they aren't contributing to the cause. They are whining but not helping. It's the dirty tricks of our competition. We were tanked by our former employee who took our secrets with him.

In our frustration, we blame our customers. In church, we might even design messages with a prophetic tone to get the congregation to be better, stronger, and more committed. Rather than lead people through the difficulty, we preach them through it.

Redefining

Well, it's not attendance that really matters anyway. We'd rather have a hundred mature believers than a crowd of a thousand immature believers. It doesn't matter how many are coming in our doors—what really matters is how many we are sending out our doors. We may not be selling as many, but our product is much better than the competition.

Instead of figuring out why we keep missing the target, we just move the target to the location where our arrows are landing. Rather than adopting a both/and mentality, we say it is either/or. We are tempted to say, "Either we are growing in numbers or we are growing in our faith. It can't be both. Either we are high volume or high quality. It can't be both. Either we are attractional or we are missional. It can't be both." Really? Why not? I think it is dangerous to redefine success just because we are missing the mark.

Leading

At some point, we decide to lead. We stop blaming, questioning, justifying, or redefining, and we hunker down and lead through the crisis. We figure out what is wrong and begin to fix it. We face the really tough data and talk about the facts of our situation that might be embarrassing or self-condemning. We acknowledge where we are wrong, and we get risky and determine to try some stuff to get back on track. We stick our necks out and cancel some stuff that has perceived success and add some stuff that has no historical track record. We work through the feeling of failure, the muddy conversations, and the awkward staff meetings.

We don't jump ship because the waters are suddenly rocky. No, instead we rally the troops, and we do what leaders do in times of crisis: we lead.

Sometimes we even write an entire book about our failures so others can avoid the same.[1] Failure is no fun. I recommend you avoid it at all costs. But there are times when things are not going as well as you'd like. It's natural to justify, question, blame, and redefine. But the more time you spend in those stages, the less time you will have to focus on the problem and lead your way out.

THINK ABOUT IT

1. Is an area of your organization experiencing failure right now that you are still trying to justify, question, blame, or redefine? What is it?

2. Have you adopted an either/or mentality about something when both/and would be more appropriate? How so?

CONCLUSION

LEADERSHIP GONE WRONG

WE'VE PROBABLY ALL WORKED FOR A LEADER WHO NEVER made mistakes—or rather, one who wouldn't admit to his or her own mistakes. But mistakes are a part of learning. I love to hear about the accomplishments of a successful leader, but sometimes I learn best when humble leaders are willing to share what they learned when they messed up. Here are a few notable mistakes I have under my belt:

MISTAKES I HAVE MADE	AND THESE
Jumping to a conclusion before waiting for all the information.	Not following my gut until it was way too late and I had a big problem on my hands.
Skipping the meeting before the meeting to help rally the stakeholders.	Spending too much time trying to convince people of a direction, and losing the window of opportunity to move forward.
Letting other concerns divert my focus from my ministry.	Letting my job become my mistress for a season.

Firing too slowly, convincing myself attitudes will improve or capacity and competence will increase.	Hiring too quickly when I'm desperate for a solution and I settle for any person rather than the right person.
Allowing misalignment to go unaddressed, or assuming it will get better on its own.	Releasing someone for misalignment before giving him or her an opportunity to improve.
Not speaking truth to power when I might have been the only person who could.	Speaking truth to power at the wrong time or in the wrong way.
Putting progress or projects in front of people.	Putting my relationship with someone in front of what God was calling us to do.
Becoming impatient with my leader rather than waiting on God's timing.	Not leveraging my influence with a leader who needed my encouragement and leadership to pull the trigger on a decision.
Convincing myself that every single decision is a deal breaker if it doesn't go my way.	Going through seasons of apathy where I fought for nothing and no one.
Not saying enough encouraging words to someone.	Saying only encouraging words when some correction was needed.
Keeping a dying ministry or program alive longer than I should have.	Killing a successful program that was providing more life and health in the church than I previously thought.

Not noticing small ethical lapses in someone that ultimately piled up to a huge character problem.	Blaming myself for being blind to an individual who was living a double life.
Talking someone into staying on the team when his or her heart was no longer in it.	Not using my influence to close the sale with someone God was calling to the team.
Too quickly pursuing a vision without considering the facts.	Dwelling on the facts so long that it killed the vision.
Putting a correction in an e-mail rather than talking face-to-face.	Failing to follow up a corrective conversation in writing, and then not having the documentation needed later.

I hope you can tell two things by this list. First, I'm not a perfect leader. In my thirty-plus years on this leadership journey, I've made my fair share of mistakes. If you are afraid of making mistakes, you should not be a leader. If you fear the day you have to stand in front of others and tell them you were wrong, you should pump gas or sell knives. Innate within leadership is the probability that you will make mistakes.

Second, leadership is not an exact science. If you do the same thing twice, it can be exactly right in one instance and the absolute wrong action in the next situation. Leadership requires prayer, discernment, collaboration, intuition, research, experience, confidence, self-control, and guts to take risks.

Above all, leadership requires humility. People will follow a humble leader anywhere. But a proud leader will fall soon and hard. Because of your gifting, your ability to cast vision and compel a crowd, people will say nice things about you, and the danger is you might begin to believe what people say. Pride is a dangerous trap in anyone's life, but more so in the life of a leader.

For a church leader who can rally people to a cause, the stakes are much higher. Your fall will not only mess up you and your family, it will mess up the lives of scores, perhaps hundreds, of people around you.

So lead with confidence, and lead with grace. Lead with integrity, and above all, lead with humility.

> Pride lands you flat on your face; humility prepares you for honors.
>
> Proverbs 29:23 MSG

NOTES

INTRODUCTION

1. You can read his story in the Bible's Old Testament in the book of Nehemiah.
2. Rick Warren, *The Purpose Driven Life: What on Earth Am I Here For?* (Grand Rapids: Zondervan, 2002).
3. Kent Shaffer, "The 25 Most Innovative Churches in America," *Church Relevance: Creating Relevant, Effective Ministries* (blog), as cited in *Outreach Magazine*, December 2006, http://churchrelevance.com/the-25-most-innovative-churches-in-america/.
4. Bill Hybels and Jack Welch, "Winning," Southeastern University Leadership Forum, Lakeland, FL, 2009.

PART ONE: BE A LEADER WORTH FOLLOWING

1. Granger Community Church, "Rumble Strips," Vimeo.com, October 30, 2010, http://vimeo.com/16351142.

CHAPTER 1: LIVE A LIFE WITH MARGINS

1. Mark Batterson, "10 Ways to Create Margin," *Mark Batterson* (blog), June 26, 2009, http://www.markbatterson.com/uncategorized/10-ways-to-create-margin/, emphasis in original.

CHAPTER 3: GO DARK

1. Urban Dictionary, s.v. "going dark," accessed April 14, 2014, http://www.urbandictionary.com/define.php?term=Going%20Dark&defid=1594376.

CHAPTER 6: LEAVE A LEGACY

1. Gordon MacDonald, *Ordering Your Private World* (Nashville: Thomas Nelson, 2007).
2. Oswald Chambers, "Beware of the Least Likely Temptation," *Daily Devotionals by Oswald Chambers*, April 19, 2013, http://utmost.org/beware -of-the-least-likely-temptation/.

CHAPTER 7: BE A LIFELONG LEARNER

1. John Maxwell, *21 Irrefutable Laws of Leadership* (Nashville: Thomas Nelson, 2007), 25–26.
2. The Global Leadership Summit is hosted every year in hundreds of locations around the world. See www.willowcreek.com/events/leadership for more information.
3. Charles Fishman, "No Satisfaction at Toyota," *Fast Company*, December 2006, http://www.fastcompany.com/magazine/111/open_no-satisfaction .html.

CHAPTER 8: GET NAKED

1. Patrick Lencioni, *Getting Naked: A Business Fable About Shedding the Three Fears That Sabotage Client Loyalty* (San Francisco: Jossey-Bass, 2010).
2. Patrick Lencioni, "Getting Naked," Global Leadership Summit 2011, South Barrington, IL, August 12, 2011. Visit http://www.willowcreek .com/events/leadership/ for more information on future summits.

CHAPTER 9: CONTROL YOUR CALENDAR

1. Mark Batterson, "Seven Margin Maxims," *Mark Batterson* (blog), December 30, 2009, http://www.markbatterson.com/uncategorized/seven -margin-maxims.
2. Alan Lakein, *How to Get Control of Your Time and Your Life* (New York: Signet, 1989), 11.
3. M. Scott Peck, quoted in John C. Maxwell, *The 360 Degree Leader* (Nashville: Thomas Nelson, 2011), 83.
4. John Maxwell, "Working Smart," *Leadership Wired: Because Leadership Is Influence* 2, no. 7 (June 2000), http://www.christianbook.com/html /leadership_wired/index0600.html.

CHAPTER 10: GUARD YOUR FAMILY

1. Andy Stanley, *Choosing to Cheat* (Portland: Multnomah, 2003).
2. I'm guessing the author and publisher came to the same conclusion. The

book was rereleased under the title *When Work and Family Collide* in 2011.

3. Andy Stanley, "The Greatest Leadership Decision I Ever Made," Global Leadership Summit 2006, South Barrington, IL, August 10, 2006.

4. Bill and Lynne Hybels, interview with Dave Ferguson, Exponential Conference 2012, Orlando, FL, April 26, 2012.

CHAPTER 13: BE CAREFUL WHAT YOU WISH FOR

1. Jeffrey Jones, "Americans Set 'Rich' Threshold at $150,000 in Annual Income," Gallup.com, December 8, 2011, http://www.gallup .com/poll/151427/americans-set-rich-threshold-150-000-annual -income.aspx.

2. Caitlin A. Johnson, "Cutting Through Advertising Clutter," CBSNews .com, February 11, 2009, http://www.cbsnews.com/2100-3445_162 -2015684.html.

CHAPTER 14: A RÉSUMÉ IS WORTHLESS

1. Dave Ferguson, "Where Do You Go to Get Staff?" DaveFerguson.org (blog), June 5, 2007, http://www.daveferguson.typepad.com/daveferguson /2007/06/where_do_you_go.html.

2. Tim Stevens and Tony Morgan, *Simply Strategic Stuff: Help for Leaders Drowning in the Details of Running a Church* (Loveland, CO: Group Publishing, 2003), 95–96.

CHAPTER 15: YOU CAN'T TRAIN CHARACTER

1. You want to follow all the laws that govern hiring practices for your industry and geographic location.

2. John Maxwell, *Developing the Leader Within You* (Nashville: Thomas Nelson, 2000), 43.

CHAPTER 16: SOCIAL MEDIA IS YOUR FRIEND

1. Seth Godin, "Personal Branding in the Age of Google," *Seth's Blog*, February 28, 2009, http://sethgodin.typepad.com/seths_blog/2009/02 /personal-branding-in-the-age-of-google.html.

2. Inside INdiana Business, "Study Suggests Online Impressions of Workers Are Accurate," Inside INdiana Business with Gerry Dick, February 19, 2009, http://www.insideindianabusiness.com/newsitem .asp?ID=34072.

3. Seth Godin, "Personal Branding in the Age of Google."

CHAPTER 17: HIRING FROM WITHIN

1. I have revised and expanded this chapter from Tim Stevens and Tony Morgan, *Simply Strategic Volunteers* (Loveland, CO: Group Publishing, 2004), 185–86.
2. Dave Ferguson, "Where Do You Go to Get Staff?" DaveFerguson.org, June 5, 2007, http://www.daveferguson.typepad.com/daveferguson/2007/06/where_do_you_go.html.

CHAPTER 18: FRESH EYES

1. Paul Alexander, "6 Principles of Building a Staffing Strategy," *Helping Churches Make Vision Real* (blog), April 15, 2012, http://www.paulalexanderblog.com/staffing/recruiting-and-hiring-teams-that-make-vision-real-part-4-6-principles-of-building-a-staffing-strategy/.
2. Scott Williams, "10 Reasons Why Kodak, Blackberry, Yahoo & Other Major Brands Fail," BigIsTheNewSmall.com, January 5, 2012, http://www.bigisthenewsmall.com/2012/01/05/10-reasons-why-kodak-blackberry-yahoo-other-major-brands-fail/.
3. The firm we hired was the Vanderbloemen Search Group at Vanderbloemen.com.

CHAPTER 19: QUESTIONS TO ASK

1. These questions come from my own experience, along with input from Melanie Rosander, Susan Chipman, Jami Ruth, *Men's Health* magazine, and ABCnews.com.

CHAPTER 20: JOB DESCRIPTIONS

1. Alexander Kjerulf, "Why Job Descriptions Are Useless," PositiveSharing.com, August 16, 2006, http://positivesharing.com/2006/08/lets-lose-the-job-descriptions.

CHAPTER 22: THE DYNAMIC TENSION BETWEEN CREATIVES AND LEADERS

1. This chapter was adapted from an article first published in the now defunct *Neue Quarterly* magazine in 2008.

CHAPTER 23: PAY WELL

1. For church salary surveys: LifeWay (compstudy.lifeway.com); National Association of Church Business Administration (ministrypay.com);

Evangelical Council for Financial Accountability (www.ecfa.org/content
/salaryintro); Leadership Network (leadnet.org/salary). For business salary
surveys: Salary.com; JobSearchIntelligence.com.

CHAPTER 25: LEAVE WELL

1. Dick Morris, interview by Piers Morgan, *Piers Morgan Show*, CNN,
February 7, 2013, http://www.cnn.com/video/data/2.0/video/bestoftv
/2013/02/07/pmt-dick-morris-on-leaving-fox.cnn.html.

PART THREE: BUILD A HEALTHY CULTURE

1. Richard Dore, "Creating Workplace Harmony," *Government News*, May
13, 2010, http://www.governmentnews.com.au/2010/05/13/article
/Creating-workplace-harmony/GQBHWNKTNZ.html.

CHAPTER 26: TEAMS TRUMP PERSONALITY

1. John C. Maxwell, "One Is Too Small a Number,"
JohnMaxwellOnLeadership.com, May 31, 2011, http://
johnmaxwellonleadership.com/2011/05/31/one-is-too-small-a-number/,
emphasis in original.
2. John C. Maxwell, "No Leader Rides Alone," JohnMaxwellOnLeadership
.com, February 28, 2011, http://johnmaxwellonleadership.com/2011/02
/28/no-leader-rides-alone/.

CHAPTER 28: ALWAYS BELIEVE THE BEST

1. Any accusation related to the abuse of children must be reported to the
appropriate authority in your state, regardless of whether you believe it to
be founded or unfounded.

CHAPTER 30: HAVE FUN

1. Barbara Harrington, "Boat Company Treats Employees and Their
Families to the Fair," WNDU.com, July 20, 2013, http://www.wndu.com
/home/headlines/Boat-company-treats-employees-and-their-families-to
-the-fair-216245331.html.

CHAPTER 31: MEETINGS THAT WORK

1. See NorthPoint.org for more information.
2. Andy Stanley, Drive Conference, North Point Community Church,
Alpharetta, GA, November 8, 2006.

CHAPTER 32: LISTEN TO YOUR TEAM

1. William C. Taylor and Polly G. LaBarre, *Mavericks at Work: Why the Most Original Minds in Business Win* (New York: HarperCollins, 2006).
2. Ibid., 111.
3. Ibid.
4. John C. Maxwell, "How Do I Maintain a Teachable Attitude?" JohnMaxwellOnLeadership.com, January 24, 2011, http://johnmaxwellonleadership.com/2011/01/24/how-do-i-maintain-a-teachable-attitude/.
5. Chip Heath and Dan Heath, *Made to Stick* (New York: Random House, 2007), 20.
6. Lucas Conley, "FastTalk: Superman Returns," FastCompany.com, July 1, 2006, http://www.fastcompany.com/57105/fast-talk-superman-returns.
7. John C. Maxwell, "How Do I Maintain a Teachable Attitude?" JohnMaxwellOnLeadership.com, January 24, 2011, http://johnmaxwellonleadership.com/2011/01/24/how-do-i-maintain-a-teachable-attitude/.

CHAPTER 33: ASK QUESTIONS

1. Marshall Goldsmith, *The Drucker Foundation: The Leader of the Future* (San Francisco: Jossey-Bass, 1997), 227.
2. Gary Cohen, *Just Ask Leadership* (New York: McGraw Hill Companies, 2009).
3. This process is unpacked with detail in my book *Vision: Lost and Found* (Charleston: CreateSpace, 2012).
4. Gary Cohen, "Leadership: How to Ask the Right Questions," BusinessWeek.com, September 29, 2009, http://www.businessweek.com/managing/content/sep2009/ca20090929_639660.htm.

CHAPTER 34: DEALING WITH MISTAKES

1. "Mistakes," *Holden Leadership Center*, University of Oregon, 2009, http://leadership.uoregon.edu/resources/exercises_tips/leadership_reflections/mistakes.

CHAPTER 37: HOURS AND FLEXIBILITY

1. Every semester I lead an Executive Pastors Coaching Network. It is for any leader who is in the number two position in leadership at a church. Learn more at LeadingSmart.com.
2. Now known as Havas Worldwide: www.havasworldwide.com.
3. Dan Schawbel, "The Beginning of the End of the 9-to-5 Workday?" Moneyland.Time.com, December 21, 2011, http://moneyland.time.com/2011/12/21/the-beginning-of-the-end-of-the-9-to-5-workday/.

4. Ibid.

5. Ibid.

6. In case you're wondering, *slacker* is defined as "someone who puts off doing things to the last minute, and when the last minutes comes, decides it wasn't all that important anyways and forgets about it," as cited in the Urban Dictionary, s.v. "slacker," accessed April 14, 2014, http://www.urbandictionary.com/define.php?term=slacker.

CHAPTER 39: IDENTIFY SILOS

1. Patrick Lencioni, *Silos, Politics and Turf Wars* (San Francisco: Jossey-Bass, 2006), 176.

2. John Kotter, "Breaking Down Silos," Forbes.com, May 3, 2011, http://www.forbes.com/sites/johnkotter/2011/05/03/breaking-down-silos/.

3. Ibid.

4. I first heard this phrase used by Bill Hybels more than a dozen years ago. I have learned a great deal from him about keeping a team focused and on mission.

CHAPTER 40: DESTROY SILOS

1. I wrote extensively about developing vision in *Vision: Lost and Found* (Charleston: CreateSpace, 2012).

2. Patrick Lencioni, 2006 Willow Creek Leadership Summit, http://leadingsmart.com/leadingsmart/2006/08/patrick-lencioni.html.

3. Jack Welch, interview by Bill Hybels, Southeastern University Leadership Forum, Lakeland, FL, 2010.

CHAPTER 41: BE A GOOD FOLLOWER

1. Mike Bonem and Roger Patterson, *Leading from the Second Chair* (San Francisco: Jossey-Bass, 2005), 11.

PART FOUR: LEAD CONFIDENTLY THROUGH A CRISIS

1. John C. Maxwell, "Leadership in Tough Times," *Maximum Impact Club*, vol. 13, no. 11, August 2009.

CHAPTER 43: LEADING CHANGE

1. Tim Stevens, *Vision: Lost and Found* (Charleston: CreateSpace, 2012).

2. Scott Wilson, *Steering Through Chaos* (Grand Rapids: Zondervan, 2010), 66–67.

3. Steven Furtick, "Sun Stand Still," Elevationchurch.org, 2010, http://elevationchurch.org/sermons/sun-stand-still.

4. Jack Welch, interview by Bill Hybels, Southeastern University Leadership Forum, Lakeland, FL, 2010.

CHAPTER 44: COUNT THE YES VOTES

1. I worked with Nancy in the late eighties and early nineties. She has touched millions of lives through her *Revive Our Hearts* radio program: https://www.reviveourhearts.com/about-us/nancy-leigh -demoss/.

CHAPTER 45: RESIGNATIONS AND CHARACTER ISSUES

1. Bill Hybels, *Holy Discontent* (Grand Rapids: Zondervan, 2007).
2. Tim Stevens and Tony Morgan, *Simply Strategic Stuff: Help for Leaders Drowning in the Details of Running a Church* (Loveland, CO: Group Publishing, 2003).
3. Ibid., 95–96.

CHAPTER 46: BAD ATTITUDES AND LIMITED CAPACITY

1. Bill and Lynne Hybels, interview with Dave Ferguson, Exponential Conference 2012, Orlando, FL, April 26, 2012.

CHAPTER 47: UNAVOIDABLE LAYOFFS

1. Jennifer Steinhauer, "As Industries Dry Up, Frustration and Despair," NewYorkTimes.com, October 11, 2008, http://www.nytimes.com/2008 /10/12/us/politics/12indiana.html.

CHAPTER 48: COMMUNICATION IS KEY

1. I first wrote on this topic in an excerpt for Scott Wilson's book *Steering Through Chaos: Mapping a Clear Direction for Your Church in the Midst of Transition and Change* (Grand Rapids: Zondervan, 2010). I highly recommend Scott's book for further insight on leading and communicating through chaotic times.

CHAPTER 49: GO OFF-LINE

1. Tim Stevens and Tony Morgan, *Simply Strategic Stuff* (Loveland, CO: Group Publishing, 2003), 178–79.
2. Tim Sanders, "Take Your Worst Business Relationship Offline," *Sanders Says* (blog), February 19, 2007, http://sanderssays.typepad.com/sanders _says/2007/02/take_your_worst.html.
3. Learn more about habit five of *The 7 Habits of Highly Effective People* by Stephen Covey at https://www.stephencovey.com/7habits/7habits -habit5.php.

CHAPTER 50: THE PAIN OF GROWTH

1. Dan Heath and Chip Heath, "Why Your Gut Is More Ethical Than Your Brain," FastCompany.com, July 1, 2009, http://www.fastcompany.com /1297926/why-your-gut-more-ethical-your-brain.

CHAPTER 51: WORK ON ALIGNMENT

1. Tim Stevens and Tony Morgan, *Simply Strategic Volunteers* (Loveland, CO: Group Publishing, 2004), chapter 62.

2. Read more about these quadrants from the Ken Blanchard Companies, "Creating a High-Performance, Values-Aligned Culture," 2010, http://www .kenblanchard.com/img/pub/Blanchard_Creating_a_High_Performance _Values-Aligned_Culture.pdf.

CHAPTER 52: THE FIVE STAGES OF FAILURE

1. The first 60 percent of *Vision: Lost and Found* (Charleston: CreateSpace, 2012) is the story of how we lost our vision during my time at Granger Community Church and got stuck for a few years.

ABOUT THE AUTHOR

TIM STEVENS IS A TEAM LEADER WITH THE VANDERBLOEMEN Search Group, an executive search firm that helps churches and ministries find great leaders. Previously he was the executive pastor at Granger Community Church in Granger, Indiana. During his twenty years there, he helped grow the church to more than 5,000 gathering weekly in three locations and saw a worldwide impact, which included a community center in downtown South Bend, Indiana, and more than 1,800 new churches in southern India.